Orioles Heroes

Remembering the Baltimore Orioles
Who Helped Make the 1960s
Baseball's *Real* Golden Age

Carroll Conklin

Bright Stone
Press
Lewis Center, Ohio

Orioles Heroes

Remembering the Baltimore Orioles Who Helped Make The 1960s Baseball's *Real* Golden Age

Carroll Conklin

Published by

Bright Stone Press

ISBN-13: 978-1484086278

ISBN-10: 1484086279

Photo Credits –
Front & Back Covers – **Topps Chewing Gum Inc.**
Topps Chewing Gum Inc. – 6, 8, 9, 10, 11, 12, 13, 14, 16, 17, 19, 21, 22, 24, 25, 26, 27, 29, 30, 34, 35, 37, 38, 39, 40, 41, 42, 43, 45, 47, 48, 49, 50, 51, 52, 53, 55, 58, 59, 61, 62, 63, 64, 65, 66, 68, 69, 70, 71, 73, 75, 76, 77, 78, 79, 80, 81, 82, 83, 84, 85, 86, 87, 89, 90, 91, 92, 93, 95, 96, 100, 101, 103, 104, 105, 106, 107, 109, 111, 112
Baseball Digest – 44, 64

Contents

Foreword

Why We Still Care About the Baseball Heroes of the 1960s.

These were the heroes who owned the summers of the 1960s.

They were special players at a special time ... when the rules were the same for both leagues, and the only thing that truly separated the American League from the National League was pride.

They played in a decade when greatness flourished ... when some of the game's best hurlers dominated in their prime, and when emerging future pitching stars were just beginning to show the promise that would lead, for some, to Cooperstown. When some of the game's best-ever power hitters smashed fences and records despite having to bat against the best collective pitching baseball had seen since the end of the deadball era.

These were the summers of the 1960s, when the heroes of Baltimore wore Orioles uniforms. On their best days (which were, admittedly, too few before 1966), they were both entertaining and inspiring. They smote hated rivals and sent their best to the All-Star game, when those games really were classics, fueled by pride and by knowing that the chance to prove one league's superiority came only twice a year ... in a mid-summer "exhibition" and in the World Series.

On their worst days, they broke our hearts, squandering late-inning leads and pre-season hopes.

They were the heroes of our youth. Powell and Pappas. Barber and Blefary. Brooks and Frank Robinson. Aparicio and Blair.

And of course, there were heroes that only Orioles fans could truly appreciate and cherish. Players like Jim Gentile and Wally Bunker and Jackie Brandt.

Players lost in the past, but never really forgotten.

Enjoy the memories.

April 9, 2013

Orioles Managers of the 1960s

Paul Richards	1955–1961
Lum Harris	1961
Billy Hitchcock	1962–1963
Hank Bauer	1964–1968
Earl Weaver	1968–1982

Paul Richards

Billy Hitchcock

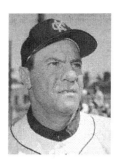

Hank Bauer

The Infielders

Jerry Adair

Jerry Adair played in the major leagues for 13 seasons. He was known for excellent defense and his toughness, especially as an out in clutch situations and as a player who was lineup-ready day in and day out.

Adair was signed by the Baltimore Orioles in 1958 off the campus of Oklahoma State University. He appeared in 11 games with the Orioles at the end of that season, batting .105, and appeared in 12 games at the end of the 1959 season, batting .314.

Adair made the Orioles' roster for keeps in 1961, batting .264 with 9 home runs and 37 RBIs. He was the Orioles' everyday second baseman for 6 seasons. Adair's best year came in 1965, when he batted .259 with 7 home runs and 66 RBIs. He led American League second basemen in fielding percentage in both 1964 and 1965, and set records in 1965 for consecutive errorless games by a second baseman (89) and consecutive chances handled without an error (458).

In June of 1966, Adair was traded to the Chicago White Sox for Eddie Fisher. He batted .243 for Chicago over the rest of that season, and a June later was traded to the Boston Red Sox for reliever Don McMahon. He was an important pickup for the Red Sox in their 1967 pennant push, batting .291 with 13 doubles and 26 RBIs in 89 games with Boston.

Adair hit .216 for the Red Sox in 1968, and then was selected by the Kansas City Royals in the expansion draft. He batted .250 for Kansas City in 1969, and drove in 48 runs, the second highest total of his career. He played in 7 games for the Royals in 1970 before being released. He retired as a player after a season in Japan.

Adair batted .254 for his career with 1,022 hits. His only post-season appearance came in 1967, when he batted .125 for Boston in the 1968 World Series.

Jerry Adair
Batted .258 in 9 seasons with the Orioles.

Luis Aparicio

In the 6 years before Maury Wills "resurrected" the stolen base as an offensive weapon, another shortstop was using the stolen base – and two of the surest hands in baseball – in launching a career that led straight to Cooperstown.

Speed and defense made Luis Aparicio the American League's premier shortstop from the mid-1950s to the mid-1960s. His impact on the league was almost immediate. A native of Venezuela, Aparicio was signed by the White Sox as an amateur free agent in 1954 and was Chicago's starting shortstop in his rookie season two years later. The year, 1956, marked the first of 9 consecutive years when Aparicio led the American League in steals (with a career high of 57 in 1964). He was selected as Rookie of the Year for the 1956 season.

As the team's lead-off hitter, Aparicio was the spark plug for the White Sox offense until he was traded to the Baltimore Orioles prior to the 1963 season (in a deal that included Ron Hansen and future Hall of Fame reliever Hoyt Wilhelm). He played for the Orioles for 5 years, leading the league twice in stolen bases and winning 2 of his 9 Gold Gloves during his tenure in Baltimore. Aparicio was traded back to the White Sox before the 1968 season, closing out the 1960s with the Pale Hose. Aparicio retired after the 1973 season, his third with the Boston Red Sox.

An 11-time All-Star, Aparicio collected 2,677 hits on a career batting average of .262, with a total of 506 stolen bases. The 342 bases

Luis Aparicio stole during the 1960s ranks him first among American League base stealers during that decade.

Aparicio played more games at shortstop than any other player in major league history (2,581) and retired with more assists (8,016) than any other shortstop in history. (Today he still ranks second in this category behind Ozzie Smith.) He was elected to the Baseball Hall of Fame in 1984, the first native of Venezuela to be so honored.

Luis Aparicio

**Number 11 led the
American League in stolen
bases from 1956-1964**

Jim Gentile

Only 12 major league batters have hit 2 grand slams in the same game, with only 2 having hit consecutive grand slammers. The first hitter to do it was Baltimore Orioles first baseman Jim Gentile on May 9, 1961 in Metropolitan Stadium against the hometown Minnesota Twins. (The other player to do it was Robin Ventura in 1995.)

Gentile was the power in the heart of the Orioles lineup in the early 1960s. Signed by the Brooklyn Dodgers as an amateur free agent in 1952, Gentile toiled in the Dodger farm system throughout the 1950s, appearing in only 16 games with the Dodgers in 1957 and 1958. In 1959 he was traded to the Baltimore Orioles. As a rookie in 1960, Gentile hit 21 home runs with 98 RBIs for the O's. He finished second in the Rookie-of-the-Year voting (to teammate Ron Hansen).

Gentile had his career season in 1962: a .302 batting average with 46 home runs and 141 RBIs. His back-to-back grand slams on May 9 came in the first and second innings. Both of those slams came off Twins starter Pedro Ramos. Gentile added a sacrifice fly in the eighth inning for a 9-RBI day.

Gentile's offensive numbers declined steadily over the next 3 years. His home run output dropped to 33 in 1962 and 24 in 1963. He was traded to the Kansas City Athletics for first baseman Norm Siebern, and responded with a 28 home run season in 1964. But over the next 2 seasons, playing for 3 different teams, Gentile hit only 26 homers, and was out of organized baseball by 1967.

Jim Gentile

In one game in 1962, Gentile hit 4 home runs with 9 RBIs.

Ron Hansen

He didn't look like your typical 1960s-era shortstop. At 6-3 and 200 pounds, he was bigger than most of his infield contemporaries. But Ron Hansen's size compromised nothing in terms of his quickness and grace in gobbling ground balls. He was as fluid and graceful as any shortstop of his time, and he was blessed with plenty of zip in his throws across the infield. His size actually enhanced his defensive range, and made virtually any ground ball hit to his side of the diamond a more-than-likely out.

Ron Hansen in the field was a day-to-day clinic on how to play shortstop. And early in his career, his bat was a threat that made his defensive abilities all that much more valuable.

Hansen was signed by the Baltimore Orioles in 1956 and made his way to the Orioles' everyday shortstop job by 1960. His anointment as the O's starting shortstop was delayed by at least 2 years due to a slipped disk. Chronic back ailments would haunt him throughout his career.

The Orioles of the 1960 season were considered on the verge of greatness, a contender built on the foundation of young arms like those belonging to Steve Barber and Chuck Estrada. Hansen's defense was integral to the success of that young pitching staff, and in his rookie year he provided plenty of offense to complement his amazing arm and glove: 22 doubles and 22 home runs with 86 RBIs and a .255 batting average. He was selected for the All-Star team and was chosen as American League Rookie of the Year.

It was an indication of the player Hansen could be during an injury-free season. Unfortunately, he had few such seasons left in his career.

His power numbers dropped slightly in 1961 (13 doubles, 12 home runs, 51 RBIs) but he led all American League shortstops in double plays. He played in only 71 games in 1962 due to military service, and re-injured his back while serving in the Marines.

In January of 1963, Hansen was part of a blockbuster trade between the Orioles and the Chicago White Sox. The Orioles sent Hansen, Dave Nicholson, Pete Ward and Hoyt Wilhelm to the White Sox for Luis Aparicio and Al Smith. In 1963, Hansen hit only .226 but drove in 67 runs. He had one of his best seasons in 1964, batting .261 with 25 doubles, 20 home runs and 68 RBIs. He also led the league's shortstops in double plays and assists.

In 1965, Hansen was healthy enough to lead the league with 162 games played. He also drove in 66 runs. Back problems limited him to only 23 games in 1966, and he was able to recover from back surgery and play a full season in 1967. But his hitting would never again match the productivity of his earlier years.

Before the 1968 season, Hansen was traded to the Washington Senators for infielder Tim Cullen. He hit only .185 for the Senators. However, on July 30 he completed the first unassisted triple play in the American League in more than 40 years. Two days later he hit a grand slam. The next day he was traded back to the White Sox ... for Tim Cullen, the first time in major league history that 2 players had been traded and re-traded for each other in the same season.

Hansen's return to Chicago had been preceded by the return of Aparicio, and Hansen was relegated to back-up duty in the infield. He was essentially a utility infielder for the rest of his career, which lasted one more season in Chicago, plus 2 seasons with the New York Yankees. He was signed by the Kansas City Royals just prior to the 1972 season, and retired after being released midway through that season.

Woodie Held

Coming out of an era when "good field, no hit" was the acceptable standard for most major league shortstops, Woodie Held was the epitome of the power-hitting shortstop, surpassed among his contemporaries only by Ernie Banks. He was the first Cleveland Indians shortstop to hit 20 or more home runs in 3 consecutive seasons. He hit more than 10 home runs in 7 consecutive seasons.

Held was originally signed by the New York Yankees in 1951 and spent more than 6 years in the Yankees' farm system, making only token appearances in New York. In June of 1957, he was traded (with Billy Martin and Ralph Terry) to the Kansas City Athletics. Held

moved into the starting center fielder role, batting .239 with 20 home runs and 50 RBIs.

He stayed in Kansas City for one season, traded (with Vic Power) to the Cleveland Indians in the deal that brought Roger Maris to the A's. Held shifted to shortstop for the Tribe and struggled at the plate, hitting a combined .204 with 7 home runs and 33 RBIs in 1958. His hitting improved dramatically in 1959, batting .251 with 29 home runs and 71 RBIs. Held blasted 21 home runs in 1960 and 23 home runs with 78 RBIs in 1961. From 1959 through 1964, he averaged 21 home runs and 66 RBIs as Cleveland's shortstop.

Following the 1964 season, the Tribe traded Held and Bob Chance to the Washington Senators for outfielder Chuck Hinton. In 1965, he batted .247 with 16 home runs and 54 RBIs in his only season in

Washington, and then was traded again, this time to the Baltimore Orioles for John Orsino. He was used sparingly in Baltimore (82 games in 2 seasons) and was dealt to the California Angels in a trade that included pitcher Marcelino Lopez. Now in his late 30s, Held was strictly a utility infielder for the Angels and, finally, the Chicago White Sox, his team in 1968 and 1969. He retired after being released by the White Sox following the 1969 season. In 14 major league seasons, Held posted a career batting average of .240 with 179 home runs and 559 RBIs.

Woodie Held

From 1957-1964, he hit 170 home runs, more than any other American League shortstop during that period.

Dave Johnson

As the Baltimore Orioles dominated American League play for most of the late 1960s and early 1970s, second base was commanded by the superb fielding and timely hitting of Dave Johnson. His arrival (as well as that of Frank Robinson) coincided with the team's ascendency.

Johnson was signed by the Orioles in 1962 and made his debut with the major league club at the end of the 1965 season. He opened the 1966 season as Baltimore's starting second baseman, hitting for a .257 average. He finished third in the Rookie of the Year balloting behind Tommie Agee and Jim Nash. Johnson hit .286 in the 1966 World Series, as the Orioles swept the Los Angeles Dodgers.

In 1967, Johnson hit .247 with 10 home runs and 64 RBIs. He also hit 30 doubles that season, fourth highest in the American League. He followed up with a .242 batting average in 1968, and then had 3 strong offensive campaigns for the Orioles, batting .280 in 1969 (with 34 doubles, 7 home runs and 57 RBIs) and hitting .281 in 1970 (with 27 doubles, 10 home runs and 53 RBIs).

Johnson's best hitting season with Baltimore came in 1971, when he batted .282 with 26 doubles, 18 home runs and 72 RBIs. After batting only .221 in 1972, Johnson was traded to the Atlanta Braves, where he had his best season as a hitter: batting .270 with 43 home runs and 99 RBIs. He hit .251 for the Braves in 1974, and then was released at the beginning of the 1975 season. He played in Japan for 2 seasons, and then signed as a free agent with the Philadelphia Phillies in 1977. He batted .321 as a part-time player for the Phillies, and hit 2 pinch-hit grand slams for Philadelphia in 1978 before being traded to the Chicago Cubs. He finished the 1978 season with the Cubs, hitting .306 for Chicago in limited action, and retired to pursue a long career as a major league manager.

Johnson hit .261 over 13 major league seasons, with 1,252 hits and 136 home runs. He was an All-Star 4 times and won 3 Gold Gloves.

Boog Powell

Once, after striking out, a disgusted Boog Powell slammed his bat to the ground and splintered it. He was that strong, and he could be just as devastating to rival pitchers as he was to uncooperative bats. In a 17-season big league career, John Powell hit over 300 home runs and was a vital part of the Baltimore Orioles success in the late 1960s and early 1970s.

Signed by the Orioles in 1959, Powell joined the big league club for keeps as an outfielder in 1962, hitting 15 home runs and driving in 53 runs in 124 games. His .606 slugging percentage led the American League in 1964. By 1966, he had moved full-time to first base. There he helped the Orioles win the American League pennant (and was no doubt an "insurance" factor in Frank Robinson's Triple Crown that year) by hitting .287 with 34 home runs and 109 RBIs. He was slowed by injuries in 1967, but rebounded in 1968 with 22 home runs and 85 RBIs.

Powell was outstanding in the Orioles' pennant-winning 1969 season. He bashed 37 homers with 121 RBIs while hitting a career-high .304. He also hit 25 doubles with a career-best 162 hits during the season. While 1969 was his best overall season to-date, that personal best would last only one season. In 1970, Powell led the Orioles to the American League championship by hitting 35 home runs with 114 RBIs, good enough to win the Most Valuable Player award. He also hit 28 doubles and scored 82 runs in 1970. In the

1970 World Series, Powell batted .294 with a double, a pair of home runs, and 5 RBIs. He also scored 6 runs in the 5-game series.

His power numbers gradually declined over the next 4 years, hitting just 12 homers with 45 RBIs in 1974. Prior to the 1975 season, he was traded to the Cleveland Indians in a deal that brought catcher Dave Duncan to the Orioles. His power numbers resurged with Cleveland in 1975, as he batted .297 with 27 home runs and 86 RBIs. But it would be his last hurrah. After a lackluster 1976 season with the Tribe, Powell was released and signed as a free agent with the Los Angeles Dodgers for the 1977 season, his last in the majors. He hit .244 in only 41 at-bats, and retired after being released by the Dodgers.

In 17 big league seasons (4 of them All-Star seasons), Powell hit 339 home runs and drove in over 1,100 runs.

Brooks Robinson

Throughout the decade of the 1960s, Brooks Robinson was simply the best third baseman in baseball. He was a vacuum cleaner at third base. He got to every ball he should have fielded, and handled most balls that no one should have been able to get to. He was not blessed with speed, but his incredible reflexes and a strong, accurate throwing arm allowed him to turn hits into outs with amazing consistency. No wonder there were so many winning pitchers on the Orioles' staff throughout the 1960s.

Robinson had a Gold Glove for every year in the 1960s, 16 in all during his career. Before Greg Maddux, Robinson's 16 consecutive Gold Gloves was a record matched by only one other player ... pitcher Jim Kaat. Those who had the privilege of seeing Robinson at third never really had the opportunity to take his excellence for granted. He simply too often did too many things no third baseman should be able to do to allow complacency on the part of the fans. He was that good.

When Robinson retired, he held practically every career fielding record for a third baseman, including most career putouts (2,697), most career assists (6,205), most career double plays (618), and the highest fielding average (.971). In the 1970 World Series against the Cincinnati Reds, Robinson put on a line-drive killing clinic that earned him the Most Valuable Player award for that Series, which the Orioles won in 5 games.

Robinson was also a consistent batting threat in the heart of the Orioles' batting order. His best offensive year was 1964, when he won the American League Most Valuable Player award with a .317 batting average, 28 home runs and a league-leading 118 RBIs. In 1966, he drove in 100 runs for the Orioles during the team's World Championship season. He finished second in the MVP balloting that season to teammate Frank Robinson.

A 15-time All-Star, he was voted the MVP of the 1966 All-Star game. Over his 23-year career, Robinson batted .267 and averaged 76 RBIs per season. His hitting alone wouldn't have put him in the Hall of Fame. But 2 decades of consistently productive hitting, along with his spectacular fielding, did.

Brooks Robinson

Appeared in every All-Star game during the 1960s,
and was chosen as MVP for the 1966 game.

Chico Salmon

A talented utility infielder, Chico Salmon played every position in the majors except pitcher and catcher.

The Panamanian native was signed by the Washington Senators in 1959 and was acquired, in turn, by the Giants, Tigers and Braves until he was traded in 1963 to the Cleveland Indians for Mike de la Hoz. He batted .307 in his 1964 rookie season, with 17 doubles, 4 home runs and 25 RBIs in only 283 at-bats. Salmon spent 5 seasons in Cleveland, batting .252 over that period. He played full-time in 1966, batting .256 with 7 home runs and 40 RBIs, the latter both career highs.

In 1969 Salmon was selected by the Seattle Pilots in the American League expansion draft. Before he could play for Seattle, he was traded to the Baltimore Orioles for Gene Brabender and Gordy Lund. He batted a combined .237 in Baltimore, but was increasing used as a defensive replacement. He retired after being released by the Orioles in 1972. Salmon finished his 9-year career with a .249 batting average and 415 hits.

Norm Siebern

Tall, athletic and bespectacled, Norm Siebern was a solid hitter who grew up professionally in the New York Yankees organization and blossomed into an All-Star outfielder and first baseman with the Kansas City Athletics. The New York papers--and even Yankees manager Casey Stengel -- occasionally made sport of his quiet demeanor, but there was no question about the quality of his production, at bat and in the field.

Siebern was signed by the Yankees in 1951, and after 2 years in the minors and a military tour, Siebern made his debut with the

Yankees in 1956, hitting .204 in 54 games. The well-stocked Yankees outfield left no room for Siebern, so he returned to the minors in 1957, hitting .349 for Denver in the American Association, with 45 doubles, 15 triples, 24 home runs and 118 RBIs. He was named *Sporting News* Minor League Player of the Year for 1957. That performance earned Siebern a permanent place on the Yankees roster in 1958, and he responded with a .300 batting average, 14 home runs and 55 RBIs. Siebern won the Gold Glove for his left field play, but ironically, it was pair of errors in the 1958 World Series that sent him to the bench for most of that Series.

Siebern hit .271 in 1959, and after the season was traded with Hank Bauer, Don Larsen and Marv Throneberry to the Kansas City Athletics for Joe DeMaestri, Kent Hadley and Roger Maris. He hit .279 for the A's in 1960 with 19 home runs and 69 RBIs. His performance was overshadowed by the MVP season that Maris had for the Yankees.

Siebern's hitting kept improving, especially as he spent more time at first base for the A's. He batted .296 in 1961 with 36 doubles, 18 home runs and 98 RBIs. In 1962, Siebern hit .308 (fifth highest in the American League) with 25 doubles, 25 home runs and 117 RBIs (second in the AL to Harmon Killebrew's 126).

Siebern's production fell off slightly in 1963, batting .272 with 16 home runs and 83 RBIs, and after that season he was traded to the Baltimore Orioles for first baseman Jim Gentile. He hit .245 for the Orioles in 1964 with 12 home runs and 56 RBIs, and he led the majors with 106 walks. In 1965, the O's, to make room for Curt Blefary and Paul Blair, moved Boog Powell from the outfield to first base, limiting Siebern's playing time. After that season he was traded to the California Angels for Dick Simpson, whom the Orioles later packaged in the trade for Frank Robinson.

Siebern hit .247 in 1966, his only season with the Angels. He was traded to the San Francisco Giants for outfielder Len Gabrielson, and in July of 1967 was purchased by the Boston Red Sox. A part-time player for Boston, Siebern was released by the Red Sox in August of 1968 and retired. Siebern finished his 12-season career with a .272 batting average. He had 1,217 hits and 132 home runs. He was an All-Star from 1962 through 1964.

Norm Siebern
Batted .249 in 2 seasons with the Orioles.

Marv Throneberry

Marv Throneberry was signed by the New York Yankees in 1952 and, after a spectacular minor league career as one of the most feared power hitters in the American Association, Throneberry made it to the Yankees' roster in 1958 but found few opportunities to play. He

was dealt to the Kansas City Athletics in 1960 in the trade that brought Roger Maris to the Yankees, and he hit 11 home runs with 41 RBIs for the Athletics in 1960.

Throneberry was traded to the Baltimore Orioles in 1961 and joined the expansion New York Mets in 1962. He had the best season of his major league career with the Mets in 1962, batting .244 with 16 home runs and 49 RBIs. But his power potential was offset by all-too-frequent strikeouts at the plate and errors at first base. He began the 1963 season with the Mets, hitting .143 in 14 games before being sent to the minors. He would never play in the major leagues again.

Pete Ward

While it's no overstatement to say that pitching dominated the 1960s, it's just as safe to say that, in the 1960s, pitching dominated the Chicago White Sox, especially in that team's contending seasons. With solid starting arms such as Gary Peters, Joe Horlen and Juan Pizarro,

and relievers such as Hoyt Wilhelm and Eddie Fisher, the White Sox featured the league's deepest staff. And they needed it, with also one of the weakest hitting lineups in the American League.

The one "power" spot in the White Sox lineup came from a left-handed batter named Pete Ward. Ward was signed by the Baltimore Orioles in 1958 and appeared in 8 games with the Orioles at the end of 1962. That winter he was a throw-in in the blockbuster trade that brought Ron Hansen, Dave Nicholson and Hoyt Wilhelm to the White Sox for Luis Aparicio and Al Smith.

Ward replaced Smith at third base for the White Sox and made an immediate impact, beating the Detroit Tigers on Opening Day with a seventh-inning home run, the start of an 18-game hitting streak. For the season Ward hit .295, fifth in the American League, with 22 home runs, 84 RBIs, and 80 runs. He finished second in the league in total bases (289), hits (177), and doubles (34), and was named the 1963 American League Rookie of the Year.

Ward followed up in 1964 by hitting .282 with 23 home runs and 94 RBIs. An off-season auto accident led to back and neck problems that would plague him, and cut his offensive productivity, for the rest of his career. He slipped to 10 home runs in 1965 and only 3 in 1966. He made something of a comeback in 1967 with 18 home runs and 62 RBIs, but the weak Chicago lineup meant seeing fewer good pitches to hit. His 18 home runs led the team, with only 2 other White Sox hitting as many as 10 home runs that season. His walks increased to

61 in 1967, and then to 76 in 1968, when Ward hit .216 with 15 home runs and 50 RBIs. Lingering injuries forced Ward into a part-time role in 1969, and he spent one year as a reserve player for the New York Yankees in 1970 before retiring.

Orioles All-Stars of the 1960s

First Base:
Jim Gentile, 1960-1962
Norm Siebern, 1967
Boog Powell, 1968-1969

Second Base:
Dave Johnson, 1968-1969

Third Base:
Brooks Robinson, 1960-1969

Shortstop:
Ron Hansen, 1960
Luis Aparicio, 1963-1964

Catcher:
Andy Etchebarren, 1966-1967

Brooks Robinson
An All-Star every season
during the 1960s

Outfield:

Jackie Brandt, 1961

Frank Robinson, 1966-1967, 1969

Paul Blair, 1969

Pitcher:

Chuck Estrada, 1960

Hoyt Wilhelm, 1961-1962

Milt Pappas, 1962, 1965

Steve Barber, 1963, 1966

Dave McNally, 1969

Jackie Brandt

Hoyt Wilhelm   Milt Pappas   Steve Barber
Two-time All-Stars on the Orioles' pitching staff

The Outfielders

Paul Blair

Paul Blair was the American League's premier defensive centerfielder in the late 1960s. He played shallow center to snare line drives and cut off singles before they could turn into alley doubles. And he had the speed to play shallow and still recover on any ball hit over his head. Few batted balls ever got past Paul Blair.

Blair was originally signed by the New York Mets in 1961 and drafted by the Baltimore Orioles a year later. He made the Orioles' roster to stay in 1965 and won his first Gold Glove in 1967, the same year he led the American League with 12 triples.

Blair's best season at the plate came in 1969, when he hit .285 with 26 home runs and 76 RBIs. He also stole 20 bases and had 32 doubles that year. He won his second Gold Glove and the first of 7 more consecutive Gold Gloves he would claim. The 1969 season was also the first of Blair's 2 All-Star appearances.

With Baltimore, Blair won 2 World Series Championships, 4 American League pennants and 5 AL East titles from 1966 to 1974. Following the 1976 season, Blair, then 33, was traded to the New York Yankees for Rick Bladt and Elliott Maddox. After 2 seasons in New York, he was released by the Yankees and signed with the Cincinnati Reds, for whom he played as a defensive reserve for one season. He retired in 1980 after a brief encore with the Yankees.

Curt Blefary

Curt Blefary burst into the Baltimore Orioles' lineup in 1965 and by the end of that season walked away with the American League's Rookie of the Year honors. The outfielder arrived with a reputation for a quick bat and a quick temper, and both found a prominent role in his 8-season career.

A Brooklyn native, Blefary was signed in 1962 by the team he idolized, the New York Yankees. But he spent only one season in the Yankees' organization, selected by the Orioles as a first-year waiver pick in 1963. Joining the O's in 1965, Blefary hit .260 his rookie year with 22 home runs and 70 RBIs. He avoided the "sophomore jinx" in 1966 by posting similar hitting numbers, batting .255 with 23 home runs and 64 RBIs. He was an important middle-of-the-order bat behind Frank Robinson, Boog Powell and Brooks Robinson, and played a key role for Baltimore's 1966 World Series champs.

Blefary hit only .242 in 1967, but still whacked 22 homers with a career-best 81 runs batted in. He was, however, something of a liability in the field, and the Orioles began experimenting with him at first base and even catcher. Blefary later attributed the decline in his offensive output to being shuttled between positions. Whatever the cause, his power numbers dropped dramatically in 1968 and would never return to the levels of his first 3 seasons. He batted only .200 in 1968, with 15 home runs and 39 RBIs, and was traded to the Houston Astros in the deal that brought Mike Cuellar to Baltimore.

Blefary's bat rebounded in Houston, as he hit .253 for the Astros in 1969 with 12 home runs and 67 RBIs. But he would hit only 18 home runs over the next 3 seasons, batting a combined .218. The Astros traded him to the Yankees for Joe Pepitone in 1970, and he made stops in Oakland and San Diego before retiring at age 28 following the 1972 season.

Blefary finished his career with a .237 batting average on 699 hits. He hit 112 home runs with 382 RBIs.

Jackie Brandt

Jackie Brandt was a multi-talented outfielder who played for 5 different teams during his 11-year major league career. His best seasons came with the Baltimore Orioles, where he was an All-Star in 1961.

Brandt was signed by the St. Louis Cardinals in 1953 and made his debut with the team in 1956. After 27 games with St. Louis, he was traded (with Red Schoendienst) to the New York Giants, batting .299 in 98 games for the Giants with 11 home runs and 47 runs batted in.

He spent 1957 and most of the 1958 season in military service, and then hit .270 for the Giants in 1959. He also won a Gold Glove that year.

Following the 1959 season, Brandt was traded with Gordon Jones and Roger McCardell to the Baltimore Orioles for Billy Loes and Billy O'Dell. He batted .254 with the Orioles in 1960, and then had his best season at the plate in 1961, hitting .297 with 16 home runs and 72 RBIs and being named to the American League All-Star team.

Brandt batted .255 in 1962, with career highs in doubles (29), home runs (19) and RBIs (75). In his 6 seasons with the Orioles, Brandt hit a combined .258 and averaged 14 home runs and 57 RBIs per season.

In December of 1965, Brandt was traded with Darold Knowles to the Philadelphia Phillies for Jack Baldschun. Now 32, he appeared in only 82 games with the Phillies in 1966, batting .250 with one home run and 15 RBIs. He split the 1967 season between the Phillies and the Houston Astros, batting .213 in 57 games. He retired after the 1967 season. Brandt had a career batting average of .262 on 1,020 hits, including 175 doubles and 112 home runs.

Jackie Brandt
Batted .258 in 6 seasons as an Orioles outfielder

Don Buford

Don Buford combined speed and bat control to end his 9-year major league career as the player least likely to hit into a double play among *all* players in major league history. In 4,553 official at-bats, Buford grounded into double plays only 34 times in his *career*. He averaged only one groundout double play for every 138 at-bats.

Buford not only knew how to stay out of trouble, but he made trouble for nearly a decade of opposing American League pitchers. A dual-sport star (football and baseball) at the University of Southern California, Buford was signed by the Chicago White Sox in 1959. After leading the International League in hitting in 1963, Buford made the White Sox squad in 1964, hitting .262 as the team's second baseman.

Buford batted .283 in 1965, then moved to third base, hitting .244 in 1966. That season, he had a career high in stolen bases (his 51 steals put him second in the American League to Bert Campaneris). His 52 RBIs were second on the team to Tommie Agee (with 86).

After hitting .241 in 1967, Buford was traded with Bruce Howard and Roger Nelson to the Baltimore Orioles for Luis Aparicio, John Matias and Russ Snyder. In Baltimore, his offensive numbers improved dramatically, thanks in part to the improved quality of the hitting that followed him in the Orioles batting order. Buford hit .282 with 15 home runs and 46 runs batted in while playing both infield and outfield positions for the Orioles in 1968.

In 1969, he hit .291 with 11 home runs and 64 RBIs as the Orioles' lead-off hitter. From 1969 through 1971, he scored 99 runs each season, leading the league in runs scored in 1971. That same season, he batted .290 and had a career-high 19 home runs with 54 RBIs. He was also an All-Star that season.

Buford played one more season, batting .206 in 1972 and then played for 4 seasons in Japan. In 10 major league seasons, Buford batted .264 with 1,203 hits.

Gino Cimoli

Gino Cimoli was a much-traveled and much-valued outfielder who played from the mid-1950s to the mid-1960s. He played for 7 different major league clubs in a 10-year career, the valuable reserve who could play any of the outfield positions and cause problems for opposing pitchers when he came to the plate.

Cimoli was signed by the Brooklyn Dodgers in 1949 and made his major league debut in 1956. In 1957 he hit .293 for the Dodgers with 10 home runs and 57 RBIs. He was a member of the National League All-Star team that season.

Cimoli's first "move" as a major leaguer was with the Dodgers, going with the team to Los Angeles for the 1958 season and being the first major league player to bat on the West Coast when he led off on Opening Day in San Francisco. Cimoli hit .246 for the Dodgers in 1958, and was traded after the season to the St. Louis Cardinals for Wally Moon and Phil Paine.

Cimoli hit .275 for the Cardinals in 1959, with 8 home runs and 72 RBIs. Following that season, he was traded with Tom Cheney to the Pittsburgh Pirates for Ron Kline.

In Pittsburgh, Cimoli was used primarily as the team's fourth outfielder, hitting .267 with 14 doubles and 28 RBIs. He hit .250 in the 1960 World Series. During the 1961 season, the Pirates sent Cimoli to the Milwaukee Braves for Johnny Logan, and he finished the 1961 season with the Braves ... only to be selected by the Kansas City Athletics in the 1961 Rule 5 Draft.

37

Cimoli hit .275 for the A's in 1962, his best all-around season in the major leagues, as he collected 20 doubles and 10 home runs, with 71 RBIs. His 17 triples were the most in the majors in 1962. He followed with another solid year in 1963, batting .263 with 19 doubles, 11 triples and 48 RBIs. He was released by Kansas City in May of 1964 after appearing in only 4 games with the A's, and signed as a free agent with the Baltimore Orioles, batting .138 in only 38 games. He was released by Baltimore after the 1964 season and signed with the California Angels, but played in only 4 games with the Angels in 1965 before retiring. Cimoli finished his major league career with 808 hits and a .265 batting average.

Gino Cimoli

Led the major leagues in triples in 1962

Chuck Essegian

Outfielder Chuck Essegian was signed by the Philadelphia Phillies in 1957 and a year later was traded to the St. Louis Cardinals for shortstop Ruben Amaro. He played for 6 major league teams in a 6-season career.

Twice he was traded to the Kansas City Athletics: in 1961 he was traded by the Baltimore Orioles with pitcher Jerry Walker, and in 1963 he was traded by the Cleveland Indians to the A's for Jerry Walker. Essegian's best season came in 1962 when he batted .274 with 21 home runs and 50 runs batted in with the Indians. He retired after the 1963 season with a .255 career batting average.

Lenny Green

Lenny Green was good enough to forge a 12-year major league career based on speed and solid center field play. But he was not quite good enough to keep from being replaced and traded repeatedly, and often traded by a team just before it celebrated post-season success.

Green was signed by the Baltimore Orioles and made brief appearances with the team in 1957 and 1958. Two months into the 1959 season, he was traded by the Baltimore Orioles to the Washington Senators for Albie Pearson. He hit .242 for the Senators as a spare outfielder in 1959, and followed up in 1960 by batting .294 with a career-best 21 stolen bases. When the team moved to the Twin Cities, Green has his best seasons with a bat. He hit .285 in 1961 with 28 doubles, 9 home runs and 50 RBIs. He followed up in 1962 by hitting .271 with 33 doubles (eighth best in the American League), 14 home runs and 63 RBIs.

In 1963, Green lost his starting job in centerfield to Jimmie Hall. He hit .239 as a part-time player, and was traded in 1964 to the Los Angeles Angels (with first baseman Vic Power) in a deal that sent Jerry Kindall to the Twins. Before the end of the 1964 season, he was purchased by the Orioles. He hit a combined .211 for the 1964 season.

The Boston Red Sox purchased Green in 1965, and he batted .276 as Boston's starting center fielder that season. He spent one more season in Boston (batting .241 in only 85 games), before being purchased by the Detroit Tigers. He was a pinch hitter and utility outfielder for the Tigers in 1967, batting .278. Green retired after being released 6 games into the 1968 season. He finished his career with 788 hits and a .267 lifetime batting average.

He played for Minnesota, Boston and Detroit one season before each of those teams won the American League pennant. Green's career was built on speed, but repeatedly fell short in timing.

Willie Kirkland

Willie Kirkland was signed by the New York Giants in 1953 and made his major league debut with San Francisco in 1958, batting .258 with 14 home runs and 56 RBIs. He hit 22 home runs in 1959 and 21 homers in 1960, and then was traded to the Cleveland Indians for Harvey Kuenn.

Kirkland had a career-best season with the Tribe in 1961; he batted .259 with 27 home runs and 95 RBIs. Kirkland hit 21 home runs with 70 runs batted in for 1962 despite hitting only .200, and was traded to the Baltimore Orioles for Al Smith after the 1963 season. Over the next 3 seasons, Kirkland became a part-time player and pinch-hitter for the Orioles and the Washington Senators, hitting 14 home runs with 54 RBIs for Washington in 1965. He retired after 9 major league seasons with a career batting average of .240 and with 148 home runs.

Dave Nicholson

Dave Nicholson was a hard-swinging outfielder who was long on power but short on contact. He debuted with the Baltimore Orioles in 1960 and was traded in 1963 with Ron Hansen, Pete Ward and Hoyt Wilhelm to the Chicago White Sox for Luis Aparicio and Al Smith.

Nicholson had his best season in 1963 for the White Sox, posting a batting average of .229 while slugging 22 home runs with 70 runs batted in. He also set a major league record that season with 175 strikeouts. His inability to get hits – other than the occasional tape-measure home run – limited his playing time, even for the offense-starved White Sox of the mid-1960s. Nicholson hit 13 home runs in 1964 and only 2 in 1965. He was traded to the Houston Astros, where he hit 10 home runs in 1966, and then was part of the trade to the Atlanta Braves that brought Eddie Mathews to Houston.

Nicholson played in 10 games for Atlanta and then was sent to the minors, never to return to the major leagues. He finished his 7-season career with a .212 batting average and 61 home runs.

Albie Pearson

This Los Angeles Angels outfielder was the team's first "star," leading the American League by scoring 115 runs in 1962 as the franchise surprised all of baseball by finishing third in the American League in only its second year of existence.

Pearson made his major league debut with the Washington Senators in 1958, winning Rookie of the Year honors by hitting .275.

In 1959, he was traded to the Baltimore Orioles for outfielder Lenny Green.

Selected by the Angels in the 1960 expansion draft, Pearson moved immediately into the team's starting outfield. He led the team with a .288 batting average in 1961. Pearson had his best season in 1963, hitting .304 with career highs in hits (176) and RBIs (47). He was also a member of the American League All-Star team that season.

Pearson finished his career with the Angels, hitting .275 in 6 years with the team. He was released by the Angels during the 1966 season.

Frank Robinson

The 1960s witnessed the prime of outfielder Frank Robinson, one of the greatest sluggers in major league baseball history. Robinson was one of two players to win the batting Triple Crown during the 1960s, and was the first player in baseball history to be named Most Valuable Player in both the National League and the American League.

The extent of Frank Robinson's talent on the field was matched only by the intensity of his competitive nature. Whether as a player, manager or front-office executive, Frank Robinson has always been a winner who would settle for nothing less ... from himself or from his teams. His skills, matched with that determination, made him a consistent winner – if not always the most personable guy in the clubhouse – throughout his career. And when you look at his career numbers, you see that Robinson was not only one of the most talented sluggers of the 1960s, but also one of the best all-time.

Robinson came to the major leagues through the Cincinnati Reds organization. Once he made it to the big leagues in 1956, his impact was immediate, batting .290 as a rookie and leading the National League in runs scored that year with 122. He also led the league in one other category that first season: hit-by-pitches (20), a dubious honor he would repeat 6 more times in his 21-season career.

By the beginning of the 1960s, Robinson was already a star. In 1961, he batted .323 with 37 home runs and 124 RBIs as the offensive leader for the National League champion Reds. For that performance, he was named National League Most Valuable Player for 1961.

In 1962, his offensive numbers were even better: 39 home runs and 136 RBIs and a .342 batting average. He also led the major leagues in runs (134), doubles (51), and slugging percentage (.624) that year. But his offensive production dropped slightly over the next three years (averaging "only" 28 homers and 100 RBIs for those seasons). Word was leaked to the press that maybe Robinson was old for his age (29 at the time) and over the next winter the Reds shipped him to the Baltimore Orioles for pitcher Milt Pappas and two other players.

It was probably the best trade Baltimore ever made. Robinson had a monster year in 1966, winning the American League Triple Crown with a .316 batting average, 49 home runs (tops in the majors) and 122 RBIs. Robinson also led the majors in runs scored (122), total bases (367) and slugging percentage (.637). He was named American League Most Valuable Player for 1966, the first player to win that award in both leagues. That same year he led the Orioles to their first-ever American League pennant and World Series championship, as the Orioles swept the Los Angeles Dodgers in 4 games. Robinson's Game 4 solo home run – combined with Dave McNally's shutout pitching – clinched the Orioles' World Series sweep.

Frank Robinson

Among right-handed hitters, only Hank Aaron and Willie Mays have more career extra-base hits than Frank Robinson.

Due to injuries, Robinson's numbers declined in 1967 and 1968 (as did the productivity of most major league hitters during those two years – even the healthy ones). But he had another outstanding season for Baltimore in 1969, closing out the decade batting .308 with 32 homers and 100 RBIs as Baltimore claimed its second American League championship of the decade.

For the entire decade of the 1960s, Robinson hit a combined .304 while averaging 32 home runs and 101 runs per season. He was the league leader in slugging 4 times during the 1960s. He finished in the top 10 in slugging every year of that decade.

A Hall of Famer with 586 career home runs and over 1800 RBIs, Robinson closed out his playing career with the Cleveland Indians, where he was also the first African-American to manage a Major League team.

Al Smith

Outfielder Al Smith was traded 3 times during his 12-year major league career. In the first 2 of those trades, to Chicago and to Baltimore, Smith had the distinction of being traded with a future Hall of Famer. He also distinguished himself as a good hitter whose legs and bat produced plenty of runs.

Smith was signed by the Cleveland Indians in 1948 and made his debut in Cleveland in 1953, hitting .240 in 47 games. He opened the

1954 season as the Indians' starting left-fielder, batting .281 for the American League champions. He scored 101 runs and led the team in doubles with 29.

In 1955, Smith led the American League by scoring 123 runs. He batted .306 with 22 home runs and 77 RBIs, and was named to the American League All-Star team. He finished third in the Most Valuable Player balloting for that season.

Smith played 2 more seasons with the Indians and then was traded (with future Hall of Famer Early Wynn) to the Chicago White Sox for Minnie Minoso and Fred Hatfield. He struggled in his first 2 seasons in Chicago, batting .252 in 1958 and .237 in 1959. He bounced back in 1960, hitting .315 with 31 doubles, 12 home runs and 72 RBIs. In 1961, he posted the best power numbers of his career, hitting 28 home runs with 93 RBIs.

Smith's last season in Chicago was 1962, when he batted .292 with 16 home runs and 82 RBIs. In the off-season, he was traded with another future Hall of Famer, shortstop Luis Aparicio, to the

Baltimore Orioles for Ron Hansen, Dave Nicholson, Pete Ward and Hoyt Wilhelm. He batted .272 for the Orioles in 1963, but with only 10 home runs and 39 RBIs. He was involved in one more trade, returning to Cleveland in exchange for Willie Kirkland. He split the 1964 season between the Indians and the Boston Red Sox, batting a combined .176. He retired in 1964 at age 36.

Smith finished with a career batting average of .272 with 1,458 hits. He scored 843 runs with 258 doubles, 164 home runs and 676 RBIs. He was a member of the American League All-Star team twice.

Al Smith
Batted .272 in 1963, his only season with
the Orioles.

Russ Snyder

Russ Snyder could find many ways to help his team, starting with his ability to play any outfield position with equal skill. But he was more than just a defensive replacement. Snyder batted .280 or better in half of his 12 major league seasons, with a .300 or better on-base percentage in 10 of the first 11 seasons that he played.

Snyder was signed by the New York Yankees in 1953 and toiled for 6 years in the Yankees' farm system until he was acquired by the Kansas City Athletics in 1959. He opened the season with his new team and played 73 games in his rookie campaign, batting .313 and finishing third in the balloting for American League Rookie of the Year (won in 1959 by Bob Allison). He hit .260 for the A's in 1960, and after the season's end was traded with Whitey Herzog to the Baltimore Orioles for Jim Archer, Bob Boyd, Wayne Causey, Clint Courtney and Al Pilarcik.

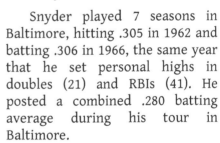

Snyder played 7 seasons in Baltimore, hitting .305 in 1962 and batting .306 in 1966, the same year that he set personal highs in doubles (21) and RBIs (41). He posted a combined .280 batting average during his tour in Baltimore.

In November of 1967, the Orioles traded Snyder with Luis Aparicio and John Matias to the Chicago White Sox for Don Buford, Bruce Howard and Roger Nelson. He played only a little more than 2 months in Chicago when he was traded to the Cleveland Indians for Leon Wagner. Snyder hit a combined .241 for Chicago and Cleveland in 1968, and then batted .248 in a full season in Cleveland for 1969. In the off-season he was traded one more time: with Max Alvis to the Milwaukee Brewers for

Frank Coggins, Roy Foster and cash. Snyder hit .232 for the Brewers in 1970, and retired with 984 hits and a career batting average of .271.

Russ Snyder
Batted .306 for the Orioles in 1966.

Carl Warwick

Carl Warwick was signed by the Brooklyn Dodgers in 1957 and made his major league debut in Los Angeles in 1961. He was traded that same season to the St. Louis Cardinals, and in 1962 batted .264 with 17 home runs and 64 RBIs combined between the Cardinals and the Houston Colt .45s.

Warwick batted .254 for Houston in 1963 and was traded back to the Cardinals, where he batted .259 in 1964 and tied a major league record with 3 pinch hits in the 1964 World Series. Warwick also played with the Baltimore Orioles and Chicago Cubs. He batted .248 during his 6-year major league career.

Gene Woodling

Outfielder Gene Woodling signed with the Cleveland Indians in 1940 and made his major league debut in 1943, appearing in 8 games before joining the military service for the next 2 years. He was traded to the Pittsburgh Pirates following the 1946 season for catcher Al Lopez, and was purchased by the New York Yankees in 1948.

Woodling played 6 seasons in New York. He had his best seasons with the Yankees in 1952 (batting .309) and in 1953 (batting .306 and leading the American League with a .429 on-base percentage). Woodling split the next 6 seasons (1955-1960) between the Indians and the Baltimore Orioles, batting a combined .285 and averaging 12 home runs and 62 runs batted in per season. He had his best overall season in 1957 with the Indians, batting .321 with 19 home runs and 78 RBIs.

He closed out his career with expansion teams, hitting .313 for the Washington Senators in 1961 and split the 1962 season between the Senators and the New York Mets, hitting .276 combined for the season. In 17 major league seasons, Woodling collected 1,585 hits with a .284 career batting average.

Orioles League Leaders & Awards

Batting Average:

1966, Frank Robinson, .316

Home Runs:

1966, Frank Robinson, 49

Runs Batted In:

Frank Robinson

American League Triple
Crown Winner in 1966

1960, Jim Gentile, 141

1964, Brooks Robinson, 118

1966, Frank Robinson, 122

Wins:

1960, Chuck Estrada, 18

Most Valuable Player:

Brooks Robinson, 1964

Frank Robinson, 1966

Brooks Robinson

American League
MVP in 1964

Rookie of the Year:

Ron Hansen, 1960

Curt Blefary, 1965

World Series MVP:

Frank Robinson, 1966

Ron Hansen
**The lanky shortstop was American League Rookie
of the Year in 1960.**

Gold Gloves:

Second Base:
Dave Johnson, 1969

Third Base:
Brooks Robinson, 1960-1969

Shortstop:
Luis Aparicio, 1964, 1966

Outfield:
Paul Blair, 1969

Brooks Robinson
During the 1960s, his glove
was pure gold.

The Catchers

Dick Brown

Dick Brown signed with the Cleveland Indians in 1953 and debuted with the Tribe in 1957. He spent 3 seasons in Cleveland as a backup, and then was traded with Don Ferrarese, Minnie Minoso and Jake Striker to the Chicago White Sox for Norm Cash, Bubba Phillips and John Romano.

Brown spent the 1960 season mostly in the minors, and then was purchased by the Milwaukee Braves, only to be traded a week later with Bill Bruton, Chuck Cottier and Terry Fox to the Detroit Tigers for a player to be named later and Frank Bolling. He had his best season with Detroit in 1961, batting .266 with 16 home runs and 45 RBIs.

After 2 seasons in Detroit, Brown was traded to the Baltimore Orioles for Whitey Herzog and Gus Triandos. He batted .244 in 3 seasons with the Orioles, and retired in 1965 with a .244 career batting average in 9 major league seasons.

Clay Dalrymple

After starting his professional playing career with the Milwaukee Braves' organization in 1959, catcher Clay Dalrymple was drafted by the Philadelphia Phillies later that year and made his major league debut with the Phillies in 1960.

He was the Phillies' every catcher from 1961 through 1968, batting .232 over that period. His best season with the Phillies came in 1962, when he batted .276 with 11 home runs and 54 RBIs.

Dalrymple was traded to the Baltimore Orioles in 1969, and spent 3 seasons in Baltimore as the backup catcher to Andy Etchebarren and Elrod Hendricks, batting .224 for the Orioles. He retired after 12 major league seasons with a career batting average of .233.

Andy Etchebarren

Andy Etchebarren was signed by the Baltimore Orioles in 1961 and became Baltimore's starting catcher in 1966, batting .221 with 11 home runs and 50 RBIs for the World Series champions. He spent 12 seasons in Baltimore, hitting a combined .232 but was valued for his abilities defensively and as a handler of pitchers.

Etchebarren was an All-Star in both 1966 and 1967. He was purchased by the California Angels in 1975, and spent his final major league season, in 1978, with the Milwaukee Brewers. Etchebarren's career batting average was .235.

Elrod Hendricks

Elrod Hendricks was an excellent defensive catcher who made his major league debut with the Baltimore Orioles in 1968. In a 12-season major league career, Hendricks spent all or part of 11 seasons with the Orioles, making short stays with the Chicago Cubs and New York Yankees.

For his career, Hendricks batted .220. His best season came in 1970, when he batted .242 for the Orioles with 12 home runs and 42 runs batted in. Hendricks led all American League catchers in fielding percentage in both 1969 and 1975.

Hobie Landrith

Hobie Landrith played for 14 seasons as a major league catcher. He signed with the Cincinnati Reds in 1948 and made his major league debut in 1950. A career backup, Landrith played for 7 different teams. His best season came in 1959 with the San Francisco Giants, when he batted .251 with 3 home runs and 29 runs batted in.

In the 1960s, Landrith played for the Giants, the New York Mets, the Baltimore Orioles and the Washington Senators. He retired after the 1963 season with 450 major league hits and a .233 career batting average.

Charlie Lau

Charlie Lau was a catcher for 11 major league seasons and for 4 different teams. He was signed by the Detroit Tigers in 1952 and made his major league debut with the Tigers in 1956.

A career backup, Lau hit .294 with the Baltimore Orioles in 1962 and .295 with the O's in 1965. He also played with the Atlanta Braves and Kansas City Athletics. After the 1967 season, he retired as a player with a .255 career batting average. Following his playing career, he became a highly influential hitting coach.

John Orsino

John Orsino played for 3 teams during his 7-year major league career. He was signed by the New York Giants in 1957 and made his major league debut in San Francisco in 1961, batting .277 with 4 home runs and 12 RBIs in 25 games.

In 1962 Orsino was traded with Mike McCormick and Stu Miller to the Baltimore Orioles, batting .272 in 1963 with 19 home runs and 56 RBIs. He hit over 17 home runs over the next 2 seasons and was traded in 1965 to the Washington Senators for Woodie Held. Orsino appeared in only 14 games for the Senators over the next 2 seasons and retired in 1967 with a .249 career batting average.

Gus Triandos

Gus Triandos was a power-hitting catcher who played for 5 teams during a 13-year major league career. He was signed by the New York Yankees in 1948 and was traded to the Baltimore Orioles in 1955. His

best season in Baltimore came in 1958, when he hit .245 with 30 home runs and 79 runs batted in. He knocked in 88 runs in 1956.

After 8 seasons with the Orioles, Triandos made single-season stops in Detroit, Philadelphia and Houston before retiring at the end of the 1965 season. Triandos finished his career with a .244 batting average and 167 home runs. He was a 3-time All-Star while playing for the Orioles.

Orioles Team Leaders of the 1960s

Batting Average:

.317, Brooks Robinson, 1964

.316, Frank Robinson, 1966

.311, Frank Robinson, 1967

.308, Frank Robinson, 1969

.305, Russ Snyder, 1963

Brooks Robinson

Home Runs:

49, Frank Robinson, 1966

46, Jim Gentile, 1961

39, Boog Powell, 1964

37, Boog Powell, 1969

34, Boog Powell, 1966

Boog Powell

Runs Batted In:

141, Jim Gentile, 1961

122, Frank Robinson, 1966

121, Boog Powell, 1969

118, Brooks Robinson, 1964

109, Boog Powell, 1966

Jim Gentile

Wins:

23, Mike Cuellar, 1969

22, Dave McNally, 1968

20, Dave McNally, 1969

20, Steve Barber, 1963

19, Wally Bunker, 1964

Strikeouts:

202, Dave McNally, 1968

193, Tom Phoebus, 1968

182, Mike Cuellar, 1969

180, Steve Barber, 1963

179, Tom Phoebus, 1967

Steve Barber

Earned Run Average:

1.95, Dave McNally, 1968

2.34, Jim Palmer, 1969

2.38, Mike Cuellar, 1969

2.60, Milt Pappas, 1965

2.69, Steve Barber, 1965

2.69, Wally Bunker, 1964

Milt Pappas, Jack Fisher, Jerry Walker

The Pitchers

Steve Barber

Strong left-handed starting pitching was a characteristic of the Baltimore Orioles staff throughout the 1960s. For the first half of that decade, that banner was carried by Steve Barber.

Barber was signed by the Orioles in 1957. In 1960, he joined a strong Oriole staff as the team's only left-handed starter, going 10-7 with a 3.22 ERA in helping contribute to the Orioles' second-place finish. Barber also led the league in walks with 113.

Barber became the Orioles' ace in 1961 with an 18-12 record and a 3.33 ERA. He led the American League in shutouts with 8, and led the Orioles in starts (34) and innings pitched (248). Injuries limited Barber to a 9-6 record in 1962, but he bounced back in 1963 with his best season, going 20-13 with a 2.75 ERA and a career-high 180 strikeouts.

During the next 3 years, Barber won 34 games for the Orioles. He was traded to the New York Yankees after the start of the 1967 season. He pitched for 5 more teams over the next 7 years, retiring in 1974 with a career record of 121-106 and a career ERA of 3.36.

From 1960 to 1966, Barber was one of the best left-handers in the American League, winning 91 games with a 3.07 ERA. He pitched in 2 All-Star games, and still ranks seventh all-time among Baltimore pitchers with 918 strikeouts.

Hal Brown

Hal Brown pitched for 5 different teams during a 14-year major league career. He broke in with the Chicago White Sox in 1951 and after 2 years in Chicago spent 3 seasons with the Boston Red Sox, going 11-6 in 1953.

Brown was purchased by the Baltimore Orioles in 1955 and spent the next 8 seasons in Baltimore. The knuckleballer was 11-9 in 1959 and 12-5 with a 3.06 ERA in 1960. He was purchased by the New York Yankees at the end of the 1962 season, and then was purchased by the Houston Colt .45s, going 5-11 for Houston in 1963 and 3-15 in 1964, his last season in the majors. Brown finished with a career record of 85-92 with a 3.81 ERA.

George Brunet

George Brunet was a journeyman southpaw who finally got his chance to start regularly with the California Angels in the mid-1960s. He was a consistently effective pitcher for struggling Angels teams, and his record as a starter for California reflected his team's struggles more than his own abilities.

Prior to the 1955 season, Brunet was acquired by the Kansas City Athletics from Seminole in the Sooner State League. He made his major league debut with the A's in 1956, appearing in only 10 games over the next 2 seasons. He was traded to the Milwaukee Braves in 1960, winning both decisions in only 17 appearances. He pitched in only 22 games for the Braves over 2 seasons, and then was dealt to the Houston Colt .45s, where he was 2-4 with a 4.50 ERA in 17 games, including 11 starts. In 1963 he moved from Houston to Baltimore, where he was 0-1 in 16 relief appearances. From 1956 to 1963, playing for 4 different major league teams, Brunet had compiled a record of 4-11 in only 73 appearances.

His break came in 1964 when he was purchased by the Los Angeles Angels and was put into the Angels' starting rotation, going 2-2 with a 3.61 ERA over the last 6 weeks of the 1964 season. He made 26 starts for the Angels in 1965, going 9-11 with a 2.56 ERA and 3 shutouts. He was 13-13 in 1966 with a 3.31 ERA, pitching 8 complete games with a pair of shutouts.

When Dean Chance was traded to the Minnesota Twins prior to the 1967 season, Brunet took over as the team's workhorse, pitching 250 innings in 37 starts. His record was 11-19, leading the American

League in losses in 1967 despite a respectable 3.31 ERA. He followed in 1968 with a 13-17 record on a 2.86 ERA, with 8 complete games and 5 shutouts.

During the 1969 season, Brunet's contract was purchased by the Seattle Pilots, and he compiled a combined record of 8-12 with a 4.44 ERA. He split the 1970 season between the Washington Senators and the Pittsburgh Pirates, going 9-7 with a 4.21 ERA. In January of 1971, he was traded with Matty Alou to the St. Louis Cardinals for Nelson Briles and Vic Davalillo. He was released by St. Louis after 7 appearances, and retired.

Brunet finished his 15-year career with a 69-93 record and a 3.62 ERA.

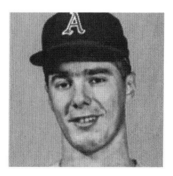

George Brunet

In 1963, his only season in Baltimore,
Brunet was 0-1 with a 5.40 ERA. He was
acq1uired by the Angels in the off-season.

Wally Bunker

The Baltimore Orioles of the early 1960s were a fountain of young pitching talent, from the likes of Chuck Estrada, Milt Pappas and Steve Barber at the beginning of the decade to later arrivals such as Jim Palmer, for whom the 1960s were a struggle until he matured into the Hall of Fame bound ace of the O's staff in the 1970s.

One of the latest of the Baltimore "Kiddie Corps" was also one of the most immediately successful. Wally Bunker was a right-handed power pitcher who was the ace of the Orioles staff at 19 and then retired from baseball by age 27.

Bunker was signed by the Orioles in 1963 and was a member of the starting rotation a year later, going 19-5 as a rookie with a 2.69 ERA. He led the American League with a .792 winning percentage and pitched a pair of one-hitters. He finished second in the balloting for American League Rookie of the Year to the Minnesota Twins outfielder (and league batting champion) Tony Oliva.

In late September of 1964, Bunker felt something give in his right arm and was never the same pitcher, plagued by consistent arm miseries for the rest of his career. He was 10-8 for the Orioles in 1965 and 10-6 for the American League champion O's in 1966. He was the winning pitcher in the third game of the 1966 World Series, beating the Los Angeles Dodgers 1-0 with a 6-hitter and outdueling Dodger lefty Claude Osteen.

Bunker struggled with arm problems over the next 2 seasons, going 3-7 in 1967 and 2-0 in only 18 appearances in 1968. He was selected by the Kansas City Royals in the 1968 expansion draft, and was the Opening Day starter, throwing the first pitch in Royals history. At 12-11, he was the team's winningest pitcher in the Royals' inaugural season, but was only 2-11 for Kansas City in 1970. He was released by the Royals after 7 appearances in 1971, going 2-3 in his final season. Bunker pitched for 9 big league seasons, posting a 60-52 record with a career earned run average of 3.51.

John Buzhardt

Right-handed pitcher John Buzhardt was a human book-end for the Philadelphia Phillies during the team's ill-fated 1961 season. Pitching for the National League's worst team (one season before the arrival of the expansion New York Mets), Buzhardt tossed a complete game 3-2 victory over the San Francisco Giants on July 28, 1961. It would be the last game the Phillies would win in nearly a month, as the team reeled off a major league record 23 consecutive losses. The pitcher who finally broke that streak was Buzhardt, who beat the Milwaukee Braves 7-4 on August 20.

Buzhardt was 6-18 for the Phillies in 1961, his second and last season in Philadelphia (he was 5-16 for the Phillies in 1960). He was traded with Charley Smith to the Chicago White Sox for Roy Sievers, and had his best seasons as a starter in Chicago.

Buzhardt began his major league career with Chicago's other team. He was signed by the Cubs in 1954 and made his debut in Chicago in 1958, going 3-0 in 6 appearances. He pitched in 31 games for the Cubs in 1959, mostly in relief, and posted a 4-5 record to go with a 4.97 ERA. That winter he was traded to the Phillies in the deal that brought Richie Ashburn to the Cubs, and returned to Chicago 2 years later in a White Sox uniform.

He was used almost exclusively as a starter for the White Sox, filling out an outstanding rotation that included Ray Herbert, Juan Pizarro, Joe Horlen and, later, Gary Peters. Buzhardt was 8-12 in 1962 and 9-4 in 1963, that season posting a 2.42 ERA. In 1964 he was 10-8 with a 2.98 ERA and in 1965 had his best season, going 13-8 with a 3.01 ERA.

Buzhardt slipped to 6-11 in 1966 and was 3-9 for the White Sox in 1967 when he was purchased by the Baltimore Orioles. He was purchased by the Houston Astros at the end of the 1967 season, and went 4-4 for the Astros in 1968 with a 3.12 ERA. He retired after the 1968 season.

Buzhardt pitched in the major leagues for 11 seasons and posted a career record of 71-96 with a 3.66 lifetime ERA. As a member of the Cubs, he pitched a one-hitter against the Phillies in 1959.

Mike Cuellar

Mike Cuellar emerged as an All-Star pitcher in the late 1960s, and then became one of the game's best starters during the first half of the 1970s.

A native of Cuba, Cuellar was originally signed by the Cincinnati Redlegs and appeared in 2 games for the Reds at the end of 1959. Cuellar spent the next five seasons pitching in the minor leagues and in Mexico, finally drifting into the St. Louis Cardinals organization and going 5-5 with a 4.50 ERA in 1964. He was used primarily as a reliever for St. Louis, making only 7 starts in his 32 appearances, and after the season was traded by the Cardinals with Ron Taylor to the Houston Astros for Chuck Taylor and Hal Woodeshick.

As a reliever for the Astros, Cuellar went 1-4 with a 3.54 ERA in 1965. But the following season Cuellar was moved into the starting rotation, and his career took off. He was 12-10 as a starter for the Astros with a 2.22 ERA in 1966, and followed up in 1967 with 16-11 record and a 3.03 ERA. He led the Astros staff in innings pitched (246.1), complete games (16), shutouts (3 – tied with Don Wilson), and strikeouts (203). Cuellar's record slipped to 8-11 in 1968 (with a 2.74 ERA), and he was traded with Elijah Johnson (minors) and Enzo Hernandez to the Baltimore Orioles for John Mason (minors) and Curt Blefary.

That trade was the best thing that happened to his career. Cuellar became the ace of the Orioles' staff, going 23-11 with a 2.38 ERA and tying for the Cy Young award with Detroit's Denny McLain. Cuellar went 24-8 for the Orioles in 1970, and 20-9 in 1971. He won 18 games in each of the next 2 seasons, and posted a 22-10 record in 1974. Overall, in his 8 seasons with the Orioles, Cuellar posted a 143-88 record for a sparkling .619 winning percentage. He averaged 18 victories per season and 3.18 earned runs per 9 innings pitched.

Cuellar was also a good-hitting pitcher, batting .115 for his hitting career (shortened by the designated hitter rule) with 7 home runs and 33 RBIs. He the first player to hit a grand slam in any League Championship Series in 1970 against the Minnesota Twins. He remains the only pitcher to hit a grand slam in any League Championship Series.

Cuellar appeared in 2 games for the California Angels in 1977 before retiring with a career record of 185-130. A 4-time All-Star, Cuellar was 4-4 pitching in 5 American League Championship Series and in 3 World Series.

Ike Delock

Ike Delock pitched for the Boston Red Sox for 11 seasons, starting in 1952. His best season with the Red Sox came in 1958, when he was 14-8 with a 3.38 ERA. He followed up in 1959 with an 11-6 season and a 2.95 ERA.

In the 1960s, Delock worked out of the Red Sox starting rotation, going 9-10 in 1960 and 6-9 in 1961. In 1963, he was released by the Red Sox and signed with the Baltimore Orioles. He went 1-3 for the Orioles before being released. He retired with a career record of 84-75 with a 4.03 ERA.

Moe Drabowsky

Moe Drabowsky and his Baltimore Orioles teammates stunned the baseball world in the autumn of 1966 when they chewed up and spit out the Los Angeles Dodgers, the reigning World Series champions. Drabowsky won Game One in dramatic fashion and set a World Series record for clutch pitching that still stands.

Drabowsky was a star pitcher for Trinity College when he was signed by the Chicago Cubs in 1956. By the next season he was a member of the Cubs' starting rotation, going 13-15 in his rookie

campaign with a 3.53 ERA. His 170 strikeouts that season were second in the league to Philadelphia's Jack Sanford.

Arm problems limited Drabowsky's effectiveness for the Cubs after that. His record slipped to 9-11 in 1958 and 5-10 in 1959. In the next 2 seasons, he pitched for 3 different teams, landing in Kansas City in 1962. He was a member of the A's bullpen through the 1965 season, compiling a record of 14-32.

Drabowsky was acquired by Baltimore at the end of 1965 and had the most productive seasons of his career coming out of the Orioles' bullpen. He went 6-0 in 1966 with a 2.81 ERA and 7 saves. In the opening game of the 1966 World Series, Drabowsky entered the game in the third inning in relief of starter Dave McNally. He issued a walk to Junior Gilliam that allowed Lou Johnson to score and cut the Orioles' lead to 4-2. But it was the last run Drabowsky would allow in that game, or that the Orioles would allow in the Series. Drabowsky struck out 11 Dodgers batters in picking up the Game One victory, a

World Series single game record for a reliever. The Orioles would shut out Los Angeles over the next 3 games to complete the sweep.

Drabowsky pitched for Baltimore for 2 more seasons, and pitched well in both of them. In 1967, he was 7-5 with 12 saves and a 1.60 ERA. In 1968 he went 4-4 with 7 saves and a 1.91 ERA.

Prior to the 1969 season, Drabowsky was selected by the Kansas City Royals in the expansion draft and spent 2 seasons with the Royals before being traded back to Baltimore, where he went 4-2 in 21 appearances with a 3.78 ERA. He spent the 1971 season with the St. Louis Cardinals, going 6-1 with 8 saves and a 3.43 ERA. He retired after splitting the 1972 season with the Cardinals and the Chicago White Sox.

Over a 17-year career with 8 different teams, Drabowsky compiled an 88-105 record with 55 career saves and a combined ERA of 3.71.

Moe Drabowsky

Was unbeaten for the Orioles in 1966, going 6-0 in the regular season and winning Game One of the World Series.

Chuck Estrada

He was a shooting star of a pitcher, bursting upon the American League as its winningest pitcher and then fading away almost as quickly. But in his first 2 major league seasons, Chuck Estrada showed a Hall of Fame promise that injury and wildness would never allow to become fulfilled.

Estrada was signed out of high school by the Milwaukee Braves in 1956. He had an outstanding first professional season, winning 17 games for Salinas in the California League. Acquired by Baltimore, Estrada spent 2 seasons in the Orioles' farm system before making his major league debut with 2 innings of one-hit relief (and 5 strikeouts) on April 21, 1960. He quickly worked his way from the Orioles' bullpen to the starting rotation, and finished the 1960 season tied for the American League lead in wins (18, tied with Cleveland's Jim Perry). In 25 starts, he pitched 12 complete games and finished with a 3.58 ERA. Estrada also led the league with the fewest (7.0) hits per 9 innings.

He followed up in 1961 with a 15-9 season and a 3.69 ERA. Again Estrada led the league with the fewest hits per 9 innings (6.8) but also led the league with the most bases on balls allowed (132). Teamed with left-hander Steve Barber (18-12 in 1961), Estrada anchored one of the best young pitching staffs in the league, one expected to allow the Orioles to challenge the New York Yankees for years to come.

It wasn't to be.

Two problems would plague Estrada for the rest of his abbreviated career: elbow miseries, and the inability to consistently throw strikes in crucial situations. Estrada's record slipped to 9-17 in 1962, as he led the league in losses though his ERA rose only to 3.83. However, in 1963 and 1964, Estrada appeared in only 25 games combined, going 6-4 with a combined ERA of 5.02. He spent a year in the minors trying to recover his pitching magic. Then Baltimore sent him to the California Angels, who promptly returned him to Baltimore 2 months later, without his having thrown a pitch for the Angels. He spent part of the next 2 seasons with the Chicago Cubs and the New York Mets, and then retired as a player in 1967 with a record of 50-44.

Chuck Estrada

His 18 wins in 1960 tied with Cleveland's Jim Perry
for the American League leadership in victories.

Eddie Fisher

Eddie Fisher was one of a handful of pioneering relief specialists whose success in the 1960s paved the way for the ultra-specialist relievers so prominent in baseball today. His success was built fundamentally on one pitch and on the advice he received from a future Hall of Famer.

Fisher was signed by the San Francisco Giants off the campus of the University of Oklahoma. In 4 minor league seasons, Fisher went 47-28 as both a starter and reliever. He made 3 short stays with the Giants from 1959 to 1961, appearing in only 35 games with a 3-8 record over those 3 seasons.

Fisher's first real opportunity came when, in November of 1961, he was traded with Bob Farley and Dom Zanni to the Chicago White Sox for Don Larsen and Billy Pierce. The trade turned out to be significant for both teams. Pierce had a 16-6 season for the Giants that included outstanding pitching in the stretch run. He and Larsen accounted for both of the San Francisco playoff victories that boosted the Giants into the World Series.

But during his first tour with the White Sox, Fisher blossomed into one of the best relievers in baseball. In 1962 and 1963, Fisher split his appearances between starting and relieving, with a combined record of 18-13 with a 3.44 ERA. During those 2 seasons, he had 4 complete games with 2 shutouts, and 5 saves.

Fisher also spent time in the Chicago bullpen with future Hall of Famer Hoyt Wilhelm. It was time well spent. Fisher perfected the art of the knuckleball under Wilhelm's tutelage, and mastered it over those 2 seasons. By 1964, Fisher started in only 2 of his 59

82

appearances, but finished 30 games and saved 9 while going 6-3 with a 3.02 ERA. In 1965, Fisher led the American League in appearances (82) and games finished (60). He won 15 games in relief while saving 24. His 2.40 ERA was second in the league to Cleveland's Sam McDowell (2.18). For the season, Fisher was selected to the American League All-tar team, and finished fourth in the balloting for Most Valuable Player.

Fisher started the 1966 season with the White Sox, but was traded to the Baltimore Orioles in June for Jerry Adair and John Riddle. He anchored the bullpen for the pennant-winning Orioles, leading the league again in appearances (67) while finishing second in games finished (50). His 19 saves (13 with Baltimore) were fifth best in the league, and Fisher completed the season with a combined ERA of 2.52. He spent one more season in Baltimore (4-3, 3.61 ERA, 1 save) and one season in Cleveland (4-2, 2.85 ERA, 4 saves). The Indians dealt Fisher to California, where he pitched for the next 4 years (21-19, 3.22 ERA, 17 saves). He closed out his career with fractions of seasons with the White Sox and St. Louis Cardinals.

Eddie Fisher
Was 9-6 with 14 saves and a 3.18 ERA in 2 seasons with the Orioles.

Jack Fisher

Right-hander Jack Fisher was 86-139 during an 11-year major league career. He played for 5 different teams.

Fisher signed with the Baltimore Orioles in 1957 and made his major league debut at age 20 in 1959, going 1-6 for the Orioles. Fisher won 12 games for the Orioles in 1960 and 10 in 1961. Following a 7-9 1962 season, he was traded to the San Francisco Giants in the deal

that brought Mike McCormick and Stu Miller to Baltimore. After going 6-10 for the Giants in 1963, he was drafted by the New York Mets and was a starter for some woeful Mets teams for the next 4 seasons, going a combined 38-73. He led all National League pitchers in losses in 1965 (8-24) and 1967 (9-18).

Fisher spent one season each with the Chicago White Sox (8-13 with a 2.99 ERA in 1968) and with the Cincinnati Reds (4-4 in 1969) before retiring. His career earned run average of 4.06 would have made him a winner with a lot of teams, but not with the Mets and White Sox of the 1960s.

Harvey Haddix

Left-hander Harvey Haddix will always be remembered best as the pitcher who carried a perfect game into the thirteenth inning in a May 25, 1959 game against the Milwaukee Braves ... a game Haddix eventually lost 1-0. Surrounding that game was a solid 14-year career as a starter and reliever for 5 different teams.

Haddix was signed by the St. Louis Cardinals in 1947 and made 7 appearances with the big league club in 1952. In 1953, the 27-year-old rookie went 20-9 for the Cardinals. His 3.06 ERA that season was

fourth best in the National League, and his 6 shutouts led the league. He followed up in 1954 with an 18-13 record (3.57 ERA), and then slipped to 12-16 in 1955.

In May of 1956, the Cardinals sent Haddix to Philadelphia in a 4-player deal. He was 22-21 in 2 seasons with Philadelphia, and then was traded to the Cincinnati Reds (for outfielder Wally Post) where he posted an 8-7 record in 1958.

Prior to the 1959 season, Haddix was traded with Smoky Burgess and Don Hoak to the Pittsburgh Pirates for Whammy Douglas, Jim Pendleton, John Powers and Frank Thomas. All 3 players going to Pittsburgh would play major roles in the Pirates' pennant-winning season of 1960.

Haddix went 12-12 for the Pirates in 1959, including his near-perfect game, which was one of the losses. In 1960, Haddix was 11-10 with a 3.97 ERA. He was the winning pitcher in 2 games of the 1960 World Series, including the epic seventh game won by the Pirates over the New York Yankees 10-9 on Bill Mazeroski's walk-off home run in the bottom of the ninth.

Haddix pitched 3 more seasons for the Pirates, going 22-16 with a 3.99 ERA. During that period, he made the transition from starting pitcher to reliever. He was acquired by the Baltimore Orioles following the 1963 season, and in the next 2 seasons made 73 appearances for the Orioles, all in relief, going 8-7 with 11 saves and a combined ERA of 2.63. He retired after the 1965 season with a career record of 136-113 and a lifetime ERA of 3.63.

A 3-time All-Star, Haddix also won 3 consecutive Gold Gloves, from 1958 to 1960.

Harvey Haddix
Posted a 2.63 ERA for the Orioles in 2 seasons
as a reliever.

Dick Hall

Dick Hall lasted 16 years as a major league reliever, pitching for 4 different teams. The right-hander was signed by the Pittsburgh Pirates in 1951 and was 6-13 with a 4.57 ERA with the Pirates, who traded him in 1959 with a player to be named later and Ken Hamlin to the Kansas City Athletics for Hal Smith. Hall was 8-13 with a 4.05 ERA in his only season with Kansas City. He was traded in 1961 to the Baltimore Orioles for Chuck Essegian and Jerry Walker.

Hall spent the next 6 seasons with Baltimore, going 44-27 with a 2.82 ERA and 48 saves. He was traded to the Philadelphia Phillies in 1966, going 14-9 with a 3.14 ERA in 2 seasons with the Phillies. Hall re-signed with the Orioles and went 21-13 with a 3.14 ERA and 10 saves in his final 3 seasons. He retired in 1971 with a career record of 93-75 with a 3.32 earned run average.

Billy Hoeft

Billy Hoeft was 97-101 in a major league career that spanned 15 seasons. He signed with the Detroit Tigers in 1950 and had become the team's left-handed ace when he went 16-7 in 1955 and 20-14 in 1956.

Hoeft became a relief specialist over the second half of his career, making stops with the Boston Red Sox, Baltimore Orioles, San Francisco Giants, Milwaukee Braves and Chicago Cubs. His best season after leaving Detroit was with the Orioles in 1961, when he went 7-4 with a 2.02 ERA as a starter-reliever.

Sam Jones

After several seasons of touring in semi-pro ball and the Negro League, Sam Jones was signed by the Cleveland Indians in 1950 at the age of 24. He made his major league debut in 1951, and played for 6 different teams during his 12-year major league career.

Jones had a sweeping curve ball to go with his fastball and change-up. He led the National League in strikeouts 3 times, and was tied for the league lead in victories in 1959 as a member of the San Francisco Giants (his 21-15 record tied him in wins with Warren Spahn and Lew Burdette). He also led the National League with a 2.83 ERA and 4 shutouts in 1959.

Jones was 18-14 for San Francisco in 1960, and then 8-8 in 1961. From 1962-1964, he played one season each with the Detroit Tigers, St. Louis Cardinals and Baltimore Orioles. His career record was 102-101 with a 3.59 ERA. He was an All-Star in 1955 and 1959.

Darold Knowles

Darold Knowles was a left-handed relief specialist who pitched for 8 teams during a 16-year major league career. Knowles signed with the Baltimore Orioles in 1961 and made his major league debut in 1965. In December of 1965, he was traded with Jackie Brandt to the Philadelphia Phillies for pitcher Jack Baldschun. Knowles appeared in 65 games for the Phillies in 1966, going 6-5 with a 3.05 ERA and 13 saves in his rookie season.

The next winter Knowles was traded to the Washington Senators for outfielder Don Lock. Knowles pitched for 4 seasons with the Senators as their bullpen ace, going 9-2 in 1969 with a 2.24 ERA and 13 saves. In 1970, Knowles pitched well but suffered through a 2-14 season despite posting a 2.04 ERA with 27 saves.

In 1971 Knowles was traded to the Oakland Athletics, where he was 19-14 in 4 seasons with a 2.99 ERA and 30 saves. He also pitched for the Chicago Cubs, St. Louis Cardinals, Montreal Expos and Texas Rangers. He retired after the 1980 season with a career record of 66-74 and a 3.12 ERA. Knowles saved 143 games and was named to the American League All-Star team in 1969.

Don Larsen

Don Larsen remains best known for pitching the first perfect game in postseason play, with a 2-0 gem over the Brooklyn Dodgers in the fifth game of the 1956 World Series. He made his major league debut in 1963 with the St. Louis Browns and, with the Browns moving to Baltimore, was 3-21 for the Orioles in 1954. He pitched for the New York Yankees from 1955 through 1959, going 11-5 in 1956 and 10-4 in 1957.

Larsen was traded to the Kansas City Athletics in the 1959 deal that brought Roger Maris to New York, and went 1-10 for the A's in 1960. He was traded to the Chicago White Sox in 1961 and after the season was dealt to the San Francisco Giants with southpaw starter Billy Pierce. Both pitchers were instrumental in helping the Giants win the 1962 National League pennant, with Larsen going 5-4 with 11 saves out of the San Francisco bullpen.

He pitched for the Houston Astros in 1964 and was traded back to the Orioles in 1965, going 1-2 in 27 games with a 2.67 ERA. He retired after appearing in 3 games with the Chicago Cubs in 1967. Larsen was 81-91 in 14 major league seasons with a 3.78 career ERA, 11 shutouts ... and a perfect game.

Marcelino Lopez

Marcelino Lopez made his way to the major leagues as a hard-throwing left-handed starter. But his biggest impact as a major leaguer was out of the bullpen.

Born in Cuba, Lopez was signed by the Philadelphia Phillies in 1959. Over the next 5 years, he won 32 games in the Phillies' farm system, working primarily as a starter. In December of 1964, he was sent to the California Angels as the player to be named later in an earlier deal that brought Vic Power to Philadelphia.

It was a career-altering change for Lopez. He started 32 games for the Angels in 1965, going 14-13 with a 2.93 ERA. He finished second in Rookie of the Year voting to Curt Blefary.

His record slipped to 7-14 in 1966, though his earned run average was only 3.93. In June of 1967, he was traded to the Baltimore Orioles for shortstop Woodie Held, but arm problems limited his role to only 4 starts for the Orioles, winning his only decision. He spent the 1968 season back in the minors, and rejoined the Orioles in 1969 as a reliever. He went 5-3 with a 4.41 ERA, and followed up in 1970 by going 1-1 for the Orioles with a 2.08 ERA. He was acquired by Milwaukee in 1971 and went 2-7 in 31 games for the Brewers.

Lopez was acquired by the Cleveland Indians in the off-season. He pitched in only 4 games for the Indians, spending most of the 1972 season in the minors. He pitched in the minor leagues through 1976 trying to mount a comeback, and retired as a player at age 32. During his 8 seasons in the major leagues, Lopez posted a 31-40 record with a 3.62 career ERA.

Mike McCormick

Mike McCormick never really lived up to the promise of his youth, when he was signed by the New York Giants as a "bonus baby" in 1956 and led the National League in earned run average by age 21. But when it seemed that his career was ready to fade into oblivion, he made a remarkable comeback that established him as the first winner of the National League Cy Young award.

McCormick went from the sand lots to the big league Giants without the benefit of minor league seasoning. He became a member of the Giants' starting rotation in 1958, winning 11 games that year

and 12 the next. In 1960, pitching for the fifth-place San Francisco Giants, McCormick won 15 games and led the National League with a 2.70 ERA.

He slipped to 13-16 in 1961 (with a 3.20 ERA), and during the Giants' pennant-winning season of 1962, arm problems caused McCormick to become the forgotten man on a strong pitching roster. He finished that year 5-5 with a 5.38 ERA in only 15 starts.

That winter, the Giants shipped McCormick (along with reliever Stu Miller and catcher John Orsino) to the Baltimore Orioles for catcher Jimmie Coker and pitchers Jack Fisher and Billy Hoeft.

The Orioles were no doubt hoping that McCormick would regain his 1960 form, but it wasn't to be. In his 2 years in Baltimore,

93

McCormick's arm troubles continued as he pitched for a combined record of 6-10 record with a 4.40 ERA in only 29 appearances (23 starts). Just prior to the 1965 season, Baltimore traded McCormick to the Washington Senators for a minor leaguer and cash. In 2 seasons with the Senators, McCormick went 19-22 with a 3.42 ERA.

The Giants re-acquired McCormick prior to the 1967 season, and it turned out to be a smart acquisition. McCormick led the league with a 22-10 record. He tossed 5 shutouts and posted a 2.85 ERA. He became the first National League Cy Young pitcher. (Prior to 1967, only one Cy Young award was made to the best major league pitcher.)

McCormick never matched that performance again, going 23-23 for the Giants over the next 2 seasons. He retired in 1971 with a 134-128 record and a 3.73 career ERA.

Mike McCormick

Struggled for 2 seasons in Baltimore between 2 tours in San Francisco, where he won the ERA crown (1960) and the Cy Young award (1967).

Dave McNally

For all but one of his 13 full seasons in the major leagues, Dave McNally pitched for one team: the Baltimore Orioles. He was on the mound when Baltimore won its first World Series, and when Al Kaline registered hit number 3,000. For nearly a decade, he was a major force

among American league pitchers. From 1968 through 1974, he won 133 games for the Orioles, and won 20 or more games 4 consecutive seasons.

He was also the only pitcher in World Series history to come to bat with the bases loaded – and hit a home run.

McNally was signed by the Orioles in 1960 and made his first appearance in an Orioles uniform at the end of the 1962 season, shutting out the Kansas City Athletics 3-0 on a 2-hitter. Over the next 3 seasons, most as a spot starter, McNally won 27 games. In 1966, as a member of the Orioles starting rotation for the full season, he went 13-6 with a 3.17 ERA. He pitched and won the fourth game of the 1966 World Series, beating Don Drysdale and the Los Angeles Dodgers 1-0 on a 2-hit shutout.

McNally broke into the 20-victory circle for the first time in 1968 when he went 22-10 with a 1.95 ERA, third best in the American League behind Luis Tiant (1.60) and Sam McDowell (1.81). He would win 20 or more games for the Orioles in each of the next 3 seasons, leading the league with 24 victories in 1970 and leading the league with an .808 winning percentage on a 21-5 record for 1971.

McNally won his last 2 decisions at the end of the 1968 season, and then went 15-0 to start the 1968 season, not losing until August. Three times in his career, he won 12 or more games in a row.

Despite posting a 2.95 ERA, McNally's won-lost record in 1972 slipped to 13-17, his first losing record since 1964. He bounced back to win 17 games in 1973 and 16 games in 1974. It would be his last season in Baltimore. In December of 1974, the Orioles traded McNally with

95

Bill Kirkpatrick and Rich Coggins to the Montreal Expos for Ken Singleton and Mike Torrez. He went 3-6 with the fledgling Expos and then retired in June of 1975.

McNally finished his career at 184-119 with a 3.24 ERA. He won 181 games for Baltimore, still the most by any Orioles left-hander. He was named to the American League All-Star team 3 times: in 1969, 1970 and 1972.

Stu Miller

He threw a pitch your grandmother could hit, or so you and your grandmother thought. But she wouldn't be able to hit Stu Miller any better than those major league batters who tried for 16 years to master Miller's temptingly slow stuff, and mostly failed.

Miller was signed by the St. Louis Cardinals in 1949. He started 11 games for the Cardinals in 1952, going 6-3 with a 2.05 ERA. He was 15-15 for the Cards over 4 seasons, used primarily as a starter, and then was traded (with pitcher Harvey Haddix) to the Philadelphia Phillies in 1956.

A 5-8 season in Philadelphia (15 starts, 2 complete games) led Miller to another trade. The Phillies sent him to the New York Giants for Jim Hearn. With the Giants, Miller continued to divide his appearances between starting and relieving, and in 1957 his 2.47 ERA led the National League. But gradually Miller was transitioned into a relief specialist, and found more success there. He made his last major league start in 1960.

In 1961, Miller made 63 appearances for the Giants, all in relief, finishing 46 games. He posted a 14-5 record with a 2.66 ERA and 17 saves, tops in the National League. It was also the year of his only All-Star appearance.

Miller spent 6 seasons with the Giants, compiling a 47-44 record with a combined 3.16 ERA. In December 1962, he was traded by the San Francisco Giants with Mike McCormick and John Orsino to the Baltimore Orioles for Jimmie Coker, Jack Fisher and Billy Hoeft. In 1963, his first season in Baltimore, Miller posted a 5-8 won-lost record with a 2.24 ERA. He led the major leagues in pitching appearances

(71), games finished (59), and saves (27). He would average 23 saves per season in his first four years with the Orioles. In 1965, Miller went 14-7 for the Birds with a 1.89 earned run average.

After 5 seasons with the Orioles, Miller was purchased by Atlanta in April of 1968. He made 2 appearances for the Braves and then retired after 16 major league seasons. Miller finished his career with a 105-103 record and a 3.24 ERA. He made 704 appearances and saved 154 games.

Stu Miller

In 5 seasons with the Orioles, Miller won 38
games, saved 100, and posed a 2.37 ERA.

John O'Donoghue

John O'Donoghue pitched for 5 different teams in a 9-season career. The left-hander made his major league debut in 1963 with the Kansas City Athletics and was 10-14 for Kansas City in 1964 with a 4.92 ERA. He was 9-18 for the A's in 1965 with a 3.95 ERA.

In 1966, O'Donoghue was traded to the Cleveland Indians for Ralph Terry. He was 6-8 for Cleveland in 1966 and 8-9 with a 3.24 ERA in 1967. He spent one season with the Baltimore Orioles, and then was traded to the Seattle Pilots in 1969. He appeared in 55 games for the Pilots, all in relief, going 2-2 with a 2.96 ERA and 6 saves. He retired after the 1971 season with the Montreal Expos, finishing with a career record of 39-55 and a 4.07 ERA.

Jim Palmer

Jim Palmer's Hall of Fame career – 19 seasons, all in a Baltimore Orioles uniform – got its start in the 1960s, and nearly ended there. While showing flashes of brilliance in his early major league career, including being the youngest pitcher to throw a World Series shutout, assorted back and arm problems nearly ended his career before he could establish himself as one of the game's most durable and consistent starters (which Palmer did during the 1970s).

Palmer was signed by the Orioles in 1963 at age 17 and made his debut with the Orioles 2 years later, going 5-4 with a 3.72 ERA in 27 appearances, all but 6 in relief. He moved into the Orioles' starting rotation in 1966, going 15-10 with a 3.46 ERA. He pitched the game that clinched the American League pennant for the Orioles, and pitched the second game of the 1966 World Series, shutting out the Dodgers 6-0 and beating Sandy Koufax (in what would turn out to be Koufax's final major league appearance).

Arm miseries plagued Palmer over the next 2 seasons. He pitched only 9 innings in 1967 and spent the entire 1968 season in minor league rehab, during which time Palmer reworked his pitching mechanics. He re-emerged in 1969 showing signs of the pitcher he would become: going 16-4 with a 2.34 ERA and 6 shutouts. He also pitched a no-hitter against the Oakland A's.

During the 1960s, Palmer hit his stride, a stride that would carry him to Cooperstown. He won 20 or more games in 8 of the next 9 seasons. He led the American League in ERA in 1973 (2.40) and in 1975 (2.09), when he led the majors in wins (23) and shutouts (10)

Palmer retired after being released by the Orioles in 1984 with a record of 268-152 and a career ERA of 2.86. He was an All-Star 6 times, and was the first American League pitcher to win 3 Cy Young awards. During his entire major league career, he never gave up a grand slam home run, or even back-to-back home runs.

Palmer remains the Orioles' all-time career leader in games pitched, innings pitched, games started, wins, shutouts and strikeouts. He was elected to the Hall of Fame in 1990, his first year of eligibility.

Milt Pappas

Milt Pappas was a solid starting pitcher throughout the 1960s. He had excellent control and a workhorse dedication. He piled up innings and wins, the kind of starting pitcher every roster needs. Yet despite 209 career victories over a 17-season career, Pappas was best remembered for being involved in a trade that broke the heart of one city, and sent another to World Series glory.

A Detroit native, Pappas was signed by the Baltimore Orioles in 1957. He made his debut with the Orioles, at age 18, in August of that season, and was promoted to Baltimore's starting rotation the next

year, winning 10 games as a 19-year-old rookie. It was the first of 11 consecutive seasons when Pappas would win 10 or more games.

He won 15 games in both 1959 and 1960, and had back-to-back 16-victory seasons in 1963 and 1964. The 1964 season was his best overall as an Oriole, finishing 16-7 with a 2.97 ERA in 251.2 innings. He pitched 13 complete games that year, 7 of them shutouts. He also struck out a career-high 157 batters against only 48 walks for the best strikeout-to-bases on balls average in the American League (3.27). Pappas was a member of the American League All-Star team in 1962 and 1965.

In 1965, his record slipped to 13-9 despite lowering his earned run average to 2.60. Then came the trade. Over the winter, the Orioles dealt Pappas, Jack Baldschun and Dick Simpson to the Cincinnati Reds for former National League Most Valuable Player Frank Robinson. The

Reds thought Robinson was on the downside of his career and were happy to get 2 established pitchers and an outfielder for him.

Pappas went 12-11 for the Reds with a 4.29 ERA. He was a disappointment for Cincinnati – a disappointment he would never overcome – especially since what the Orioles got in Robinson was the 1966 Triple Crown winner and the American League MVP – the first player to win an MVP in each league. The Orioles also happened to win the World Series that year.

Pappas pitched one more season in Cincinnati, going 16-13 with a 3.35 ERA, and the next season was dealt with Ted Davidson and Bob Johnson to the Atlanta Braves for Clay Carroll, Tony Cloninger and Woody Woodward. His combined record in 1968 was 12-13 with a 3.47 ERA. In 3 seasons with the Braves, Pappas was 18-20, and was sold to the Chicago Cubs in 1970. His career rebounded in Chicago, winning 17 games in both 1971 and 1972. He retired after the 1973 season with a career record of 209-164 and a 3.40 career ERA.

Milt Pappas
From 1959 through 1965, Pappas won 100
games for the Orioles with a 3.18 ERA.

Tom Phoebus

Tom Phoebus was a right-handed pitcher with 3 teams in 7 major league seasons. He broke into the major leagues with Baltimore in 1966 and 14-9 with a 3.33 ERA as a rookie in 1967.

Phoebus was 15-15 with a 2.62 ERA in 1968 and 14-7 with a 3.52 ERA in 1969. In 1968 he threw a 6-0 no-hitter against the Red Sox.

Phoebus was traded to San Diego in 1970 in the same deal that brought Pat Dobson to the Orioles. He finished his career with the Cubs in 1972. In a 7-year career, Phoebus compiled a 56–52 record with 725 strikeouts and a 3.33 ERA in 1,030 innings pitched.

Pete Richert

Few pitchers have had as dramatic a debut as the one that launched Pete Richert's major league career. And while the history of major league baseball is loaded with one-time wonders who burst on the scene with dazzling promise only to fade just as quickly into obscurity, Richert's dazzling start was followed by a solid and consistently productive pitching career.

Richert was signed out of high school by the Los Angeles Dodgers. He toiled in the Dodgers' farm system for 4 years, successful at every stop and even winning 19 games for Double-A Atlanta in 1960.

His major league debut came on April 12, 1962. Richert entered the game with 2 outs in the bottom of the second inning, striking out Cincinnati Reds center fielder Vada Pinson to end the inning.

In the third inning, Richert struck out the Reds ... all 4 of them. (First baseman Gordy Coleman reached first on a passed ball after striking out.) In the top of the fourth, Richert struck out the first hitter, outfielder Tommy Harper, for his sixth consecutive strikeout in what was, thus far, a 6-batter major league career. No one before Pete Richert had opened his pitching career by striking out the first 6 major league batters he faced. And no one else has done it since.

Richert's rookie season in Los Angeles resulted in a 5-4 record with a 3.87 ERA. He struck out 75 batters in 81.1 innings. Richert would win only 7 more games for the Dodgers over the next 2 seasons. Following the 1964 season, he was traded with Frank Howard, Ken McMullen and Phil Ortega to the Washington Senators for John Kennedy, Claude Osteen and $100,000. (First baseman Dick

Nen was later sent to the Senators as the player named later.) With Washington, Richert became the team's ace starter, going 15-12 (with a 2.60 ERA) in 1965 and 14-14 in 1966. He was selected for the American League All-Star team both of those seasons.

Early in the 1967 campaign, Richert was traded to the Baltimore Orioles for Frank Bertaina and Mike Epstein. During his 5-year stay in Baltimore, Richert became one of the American League's best left-handed relievers. He also pitched for the Dodgers (again), as well as for the St. Louis Cardinals and Philadelphia Phillies before retiring after the 1974 season. He finished his career at 80-73 with a combined 3.19 ERA.

Pete Richert
In 5 seasons out of the Baltimore bullpen, Richert posted a 2.83 ERA and 37 saves.

Robin Roberts

Major league baseball's second-winningest pitcher in the 1950s (3 wins behind Warren Spahn), Robin Roberts was considered washed-up – and his arm, literally, used up – as baseball entered the 1960s. Yet after starting the decade by going 13-26, he made a remarkable turn-around, posting a won-lost record of 52-46 from 1962 through 1966.

For all of his pitching tools during his string of 6 consecutive 20-victory seasons, Robin Roberts was first and foremost a heady pitcher, a guy who knew how to pitch and how to win. He relied on that savvy when his fastball was no longer intimidating, and he rode that knowledge all the way to Cooperstown.

A 2-sport athlete at Michigan State University, Roberts was signed by the Philadelphia Phillies in 1948 and made his major league debut that same season, going 7-9 with a 3.19 ERA as a 21-year-old rookie. Roberts won 15 games in 1949, and then led the Phillies to the 1950 National League pennant with a 20-11 record and a 3.02 ERA.

It was the first of 6 consecutive 20-victory seasons for Roberts. He would win 28 games in 1952 and 23 each year from 1953 through 1955. Altogether, from 1950 through 1955, Roberts won 138 games with a combined ERA of 2.93.

He won 19 games in 1956 and slipped to 10-22 in 1957. By 1960, he was still the best pitcher on baseball's worst team, going 12-16 in 1960 and 1-10 in 1961. The New York Yankees purchased Roberts following the 1961 season but released him in May of 1962, and Roberts signed with the Baltimore Orioles. He went 10-9 for the Orioles in 1962 with a 2.78 ERA, and won 14 games for Baltimore in 1963. He had his best overall season for the Orioles in 1964, going 13-7 with a 2.91 ERA and 4 shutouts.

In 1965, he won 5 games each for the Orioles and then the Houston Astros. Then he split the 1966 season between Houston and the Chicago Cubs, going 5-8. He retired after the 1966 season, his nineteenth in the big leagues.

Roberts finished his major league career with a 286-245 record and a 3.41 ERA. He led the major leagues in victories 4 times, led the National league in starts 6 times, and led the league in complete games and innings pitched 5 times. An All-Star 7 times, Roberts was inducted into the Baseball Hall of Fame in 1976.

Robin Roberts

**In 4 seasons with the Orioles, Roberts
won 42 games with a 3.09 ERA.**

Wes Stock

Wes Stock's career as a major league pitching coach lasted more than twice as long as his career as a player, but he was a consistently effective reliever for the Baltimore Orioles and Kansas City Athletics between 1961 and 1966.

The lanky Stock was signed out of Washington State University in 1956 by the Orioles. He had an outstanding first professional season, going 14-6 for Aberdeen in the Northern League. His development was suspended for 2 years of military service, and over the next 2  seasons he made limited appearances with Baltimore, posting a combined record of 2-2 with 3 saves in 24 appearances.

Stock made the Orioles roster for keeps in 1961, going 5-0 in 35 appearances with a 3.01 ERA. He appeared in exactly 100 games for the Orioles over the next 2 seasons, for a combined record of 10-2 with 4 saves and a 4.17 ERA.

In June of 1964, the Orioles traded Stock to the Kansas City Athletics for catcher Charlie Lau. The bullpen was one of the few strengths of the cellar-dwelling A's of 1964, as Stock joined Moe Drabowsky and Ted Bowsfield as set-up pitchers for A's closer John Wyatt.

Stock had an excellent remainder of the 1964 season for Kansas City. He appeared in 50 games in a little more than 3 months remaining in the season, posting a 1.94 ERA with a 6-3 record and 5 saves. Overall, 1964 was his best season, with a combined 8-3 record and 2.30 ERA for the Orioles and Athletics.

The 1965 season was not as kind to Stock, whose record fell to 0-4 with a 5.24 ERA in 62 appearances. He appeared in only 35 games in 1966, going 2-2 with a 2.66 ERA. He retired after 1 appearance in 1967, and afterward enjoyed a 2-decade career as one of the game's most respected pitching coaches.

Jerry Walker

Precocious only begins to describe the brief career of pitcher Jerry Walker. At age 20, he was the youngest player ever to start an All-Star game. By age 26, he was retired.

Walker was signed by the Baltimore Orioles in 1957 and found a spot immediately in the Orioles' bullpen, with no stops in the minor leagues. He was 1-0 as an 18-year-old rookie, with a 2.93 ERA. His only decision was a 10-inning, 4-hit shutout of the Washington Senators.

He appeared in only 6 games in 1958, and then started out 7-3 in 1959, garnering the starting assignment in that year's All-Star game. He finished the 1959 season at 11-10 with a 2.92 ERA.

The Orioles entered the 1960s with what was considered one of the best young starting rotations in baseball. Their "Kiddie Corps" included Walker, Milt Pappas, Chuck Estrada and Steve Barber. Unfortunately for Walker, he would be the first to be removed from the group.

After going 3-4 with a 3.74 ERA in 1960, Walker was traded with Chuck Essegian to the Kansas City Athletics for Dick Hall and Dick Williams. In his first season in Kansas City, Walker won 8 games for an Athletics team that finished ninth at 61-100. He won 8 more games in 1962, and then was traded to the Cleveland Indians for Chuck Essegian ... the same Chuck Essegian who accompanied him on the trade from Baltimore to Kansas City. Walker went 6-6 for the Tribe in 1963, with all but 2 of his 39 appearances coming in relief. He retired after 6 appearances in the 1964 season. He was only 25 at the time he retired. Walker finished with an 8-year career record of 37-44 and a 4.66 ERA.

Eddie Watt

A hard-throwing, right-handed relief specialist, Eddie Watt was signed by the Baltimore Orioles in 1961 and made his major league debut in 1966, going 9-7 with a 3.83 ERA as a starter-reliever. His 13 career starts all came in 1966, and he was exclusively a reliever for the rest of his career.

Watt pitched for 8 seasons with the Orioles. His best season came in 1969, when he was 5-2 with a 1.65 ERA and 16 saves. He spent one year each with the Philadelphia Phillies and Chicago Cubs before retiring after the 1975 season. In his 10-year major league career, Watt was 38-36 in 411 appearances. He posted a 2.91 ERA and 80 career saves.

Hoyt Wilhelm

It's probably the most unhittable pitch in baseball (with apologies to any pitch ever thrown by Sandy Koufax). And it may be the most unpitchable.

The knuckleball is slow, it doesn't rotate, and it doesn't offer many clues as to where it will end up. But one pitcher, more than any,  is associated with the knuckleball, and was such a master of its unpredictability that it floated him all the way to Cooperstown.

Hoyt Wilhelm broke into the major leagues with the New York Giants in 1952 as a 29-year-old rookie. That year he led the National League with a .833 winning percentage on a 15-3 record. He also led the league in games pitched (71, all in relief) and in earned run average (2.43). In his first major league at-bat, he hit a home run (the only one of his career).

For more than 2 decades thereafter, Wilhelm remained one of the game's most durable and productive relievers. He entered the 1960s in the middle of a 5-year stretch with the Baltimore Orioles. After a brief stint as a starter for the Orioles (in his first major league start, he pitched a no-hitter), Wilhelm recorded 33 saves over the next 2 years, second best in the American League to Luis Arroyo's 36. Then he was traded to the White Sox in the deal that brought Luis Aparicio to the Orioles. In 6 years with Chicago, Wilhelm appeared in 361 games for the White Sox, all but 3 as a reliever. He saved 98 games, with an ERA of 1.92 for those 6 years combined. Wilhelm closed out the 1960s by splitting the 1969 season between the California Angels and the Atlanta Braves, with a total of 14 saves and a combined ERA of 2.19.

Throughout the 1960s, no other relief pitcher was as consistently effective as Wilhelm. During those 10 years, he won 75 games and saved 152 more, with an ERA of 2.19 for the decade. His career lasted 2 years beyond the 1960s, with his retirement after the 1971 season at age 48. His 1,070 career appearances were the major league record at the time Wilhelm called it quits.

Today Wilhelm still ranks fifth in most career games by a pitcher. He remains the all-time major league leader in career wins in relief (124) and in career innings pitched in relief (1,871). Opponents' career batting average against Wilhelm was only .216, lower than batters' career averages against fellow Hall-of-Famers such as Tom Seaver (.226), Catfish Hunter (.231) and Rollie Fingers (.235). An 8-time All-Star, Wilhelm was elected to the Baseball Hall of Fame in 1985.

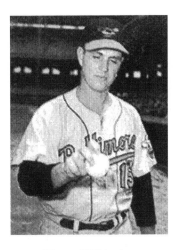

Hoyt Wilhelm
In 5 seasons with the Orioles, Wilhelm won 43
games, saved 40 and posted a 2.42 ERA.

About the Author

Carroll Conklin combines a life-long passion for baseball with a three-decade career as a professional writer.

A graduate of Ashland University and Bowling Green State University, Carroll has spent more than 20 years as an advertising copywriter and marketing strategist. He has taught copywriting and brand theory at The Ohio State University and the Columbus College of Art & Design.

A prolific author, Carroll has also written books on topics ranging from marketing management to fear elimination.

He preaches the "gospel" of the 1960s as baseball's real golden age at www.1960sBaseball.com.

33066096R00067

Made in the USA
Lexington, KY
11 June 2014